FREEDOM   LEADERSHIP   DREAMS

Coaching For High
Performance

Eighteen Essential Elements
for
Professional and Personal Coaching

By Bob Davies, M. Ed., CPPC*

*Certified professional and personal coach

Coaching for High Performance

Eighteen Essential Elements for
Professional and Personal Coaching

Bob Davies, M. Ed., CPPC

TABLE OF CONTENTS

Acknowledgments

I would like to acknowledge everyone who has had an influence on my life and has helped me to shape my coaching philosophy. Every coaching staff I have been associated with from the time I was an athlete in high school in Long Branch, New Jersey, has made a contribution. I specifically wish to mention the following: the football and wrestling staffs at Rutgers University; the staff and administration at Creskill High School in New Jersey; the football and wrestling staff at Springfield College in Massachusetts; the staff and administration who helped me with my first head coaching college experience at California Institute of Technology in Pasadena, California; and the staff, administration, and athletes at Cal State Fullerton.

Special thanks go to all of my clients, who continue to be sources of learning for me. Thank you to the founders of THE COACHES Training Institute, Laura Whitworth and Karen and Henry Kimsey House, for your help in training me and shaping my foundation so that I could arrive at the principles in this book.

I acknowledge my daughter, Danielle, a continuous fountain of love, learning, and commitment, enhancing my growth.

Most of all, I thank and acknowledge you, the reader. Thank you for having the state of mind to be interested in what this·book has to offer you as you continue on your journey to be your best.

The objective for this book is to enable you to begin the coaching process with another person immediately. It is not designed to train you to be a professional coach.

I recommend that you contact THE COACHES Training Institute for that information (415-451-6000). I also recommend that you hire a professional coach yourself. Please call my office for referrals (949-223-3704).

Preface
By Laura Whitworth, CPPC

I always appreciate the opportunity to talk about Professional and Personal Coaching. Looking back at the last eight years as a Professional and Personal Coach, I am always astonished at both the simplicity and the complexity of the coaching process. An outside observer would simply see two people talking (usually by phone): talking about the present, the future, obstacles, and creating plans of action. The complexity comes in when looking at the results of such straightforward conversation. For some clients the act of intentional conversation alone creates clarity, action, and forward momentum; for another, it is the act of accountability that makes all the difference; for yet another, the process of incorporating more balance or more self-reflection returns them to their desired outcomes.

One of the key reasons that coaching is effective, especially with the visionary and/or entrepreneurial type of clients, is the act of creating solutions and workability through talking with the coach. I have noticed that individuals, when left to their own thoughts and habits, have a tendency toward comfort, safety, and inaction. Bob Davies calls this the alien, otherwise known as the "success saboteur." When you are in a regular conversation with someone which is designed to focus only on you, on your future, on your goals and strategies, on your failures and the skills you need to develop, on holding you accountable to what you say you want— well, the outcome is a proactive life, results, and a sense of fulfillment.

While designing the Professional Coaching Course in 1993 we observed that a key element in the coaching process is the act of clarification. It is rare for an individual to seriously examine such questions as "What do you want? What do you really want, in your career, in life? What stops you from getting it? Where do you take your foot off the gas? What will you do about it? What resources or competencies must you acquire to get there? By when will you do it?" Questions such as these usually propel the client into a mode of learning, self-discovery, and effective action, action which is aligned with a successful and fulfilling life.

One of the key assumptions in coaching is that clients are naturally creative, resourceful, and whole. It is not so much that clients don't know what to do; they just don't do it. If clients really don't know what action to take, they often procrastinate in taking the steps to learn how. Once again the Alien reigns.

During the initial coaching session, clients make clear to themselves and to the coach what they want and together with the coach they design actions to move toward their outcomes. This all sounds simple, yet it is in the implementation process that things begin to break down because that process takes time.

Life is so full of constant distractions these days from the real priorities or the main focus. Distractions may look like returning the 25 voice mail messages, dealing with the flat tire, a closing deadline, handling the mail or the broken muffler, putting paper in the fax machine, learning about the internet, or the spousal demands for more family time. In essence, the main source of distraction is life itself. You may have noticed how much busier you are now than, say, 5 or 10 years ago. Life can seem like an out-of-control rollercoaster unless you work with a coach who is holding your key priorities and holding the focus on what you say is important.

I was working with a group of high level executives this week. They realize that their department is in jeopardy of being eliminated yet they are so busy handling the day-to-day tasks that they failed to be strategic and proactive in terms of the viability of the department. They know that they are metaphorically applying a band-aid to a severed limb. We set up a group coaching program that will hold their focus, no kidding, on the life-threatening priorities while proceeding to reduce the distractions and less important demands on their time. These powerful and successful people said, "We know we need to do this; we just never seem to get around to it. Sound familiar?"

In working with ReMax broker/agents I have noticed that the biggest challenge is making the time to do activities to recruit new agents. They know what to do. They know how to do it. And then life gets in the way. Somebody wants to close on a house, there are problems at the office, it is too uncomfortable to make those recruiting calls—so why not handle staff problems instead. During coaching they examine their management style and how they spend their time; then, they create specific and consistent times to focus on recruiting. This, coupled with the aid of weekly accountability and self-examination, has increased recruiting results—and the broker/agent feels good about it too.

A stockbroker client of mine exceeded his annual goal considerably through the ongoing and consistent use of our weekly coaching sessions. She left to start her own business when she got clear about what she really wanted and knew that she could do it. A recently promoted executive took his leadership skills to a new level and has begun to have fun on the job while gaining greater productivity from his staff. One client realized that a spiritual component was missing from his life—with a few revisions in his daily schedule he has become a more loving and caring father. Claude, a highly successful attorney, has refined and expanded his practice and is getting married soon; while he thanks his coach for the joy he is experiencing in life, he is the one who actually took the appropriate steps. When I asked one of my clients to keep his word for an entire week, his whole life was altered, his sense of self sky-rocketed and he eventually became president of the company, known as a man of integrity and vision. A local politician client thanked me this week when I held her to her goals (at her request) and actually feels like she may avoid killing herself with work.

These may seem like simple advancements in an individual's life—Yes, the removal of the overriding sense of dissatisfaction that allows these clients to be more effective, generous and at ease in their lives. And, oh, don't let me forget to mention that in most cases there is also a literal increase in financial wellbeing and health.

I love talking about coaching. As a Star Trek fan I often find that coaching provides an opportunity for individuals to go where they have not gone before: to a heightened ability accomplish what they want to do and to greater levels of efficiency, effectiveness, abundance and joy.

Warm regards.

Laura Whitworth, CPPC
THE COACHES Training Institute

About The Author

Bob Davies, Certified Professional and Personal coach, is a former coach at Cal State Fullerton, where his techniques helped an average football team win two conference championships.

Bob is the former coach of Olympic gold medal winner Jeff Blatnick, who overcame cancer to win the gold medal in the 1984 Olympics.

With a Masters in Psychology and a B. S. in Health, this Rutgers University graduate uses his unique coaching techniques to help entrepreneurs break through fears to plan more precisely and to create balance and fulfillment in their lives as they achieve results in very powerful ways.

Introduction

My last experience as an athletic coach was in 1983. I was an assistant football coach at Cal State Fullerton, a Division I college football program. Previously, I had been the head football and wrestling coach at California Institute of Technology in Pasadena, California, from 1979 until 1980. Prior to that I was an assistant football and wrestling coach at Springfield College, a Division III school. There I had the opportunity to coach Olympic gold medal winner Jeff Blatnick. Blatnick won the gold in the 1984 Olympics in Greco Roman Wrestling. I attended Springfield from 1977 to 1979. Before I became a college coach, I was a teacher and coach of football and wrestling at Creskill High School in Creskill, New Jersey. Before Creskill High School, I attended Rutgers University, where I played football. I also wrestled in my senior year. All these experiences have one thing in common: they involved coaching programs.

What does it mean to be in a coaching program? It ideally means that you are in contact with someone who has your best interests in mind. This person helps you define and take the action that is necessary to reach your goals.

Timothy Gallwey in his book, *The Inner Game of Tennis*, writes: *"Coaching is unlocking a person's potential to maximize his or her own performance. It is helping them to learn, rather than teaching them."*

Every great athlete has a coach. Andre Agassi or Pete Sampris, two of the world's greatest tennis players, would never attempt to perform on the elite level without having a coach. They don't need a coach to teach them how to hit a backhand. They need a coach to challenge them, to keep them looking at ways to perform at a more effective level.

There is no doubt about it. Coaching works one hundred percent of the time. I guarantee that you will always get more accomplished with a coach than you would without one.

Who needs a coach?

Coaching is not for everyone. A key word will let you know if coaching is for you. That word is SATISFIED. If you are satisfied with the results you are getting in your health, business and personal life, please buy another copy of this book and pass it on to a friend and keep one copy for yourself. Place it in your book case and remember where it is. Coaching is not for you at this time. However, some day you may not be satisfied with the results you are achieving. When you reach that state of mind, dust off this book and follow the recommendations.

For example, I am an average or "B Level" racquetball player. The ratings in racquetball are Professional or Open, A level, B level, C level and beginner or D level. I can compete against an A level player and give that player a good, competitive game. I probably won't beat the player, but we will both get a good workout. I hold my own against fellow "B level" players, beating some and losing to others. Although I am very competitive, I really don't care if I win as long as I get a good workout. I could greatly improve my game with coaching, but I am satisfied. In this area of my life, I don't need a coach.

A friend of mine, Dee, takes the court with her coach. Dee at one time was ranked twelfth in the USA in the woman's professional tour. I have never beaten her two out of three games. Rarely in fact, do I ever beat her at all. She is precise in her play and I can't afford to make one mistake against her. If you leave a ball high, she puts it away. If your serve comes off the side wall, she puts it away. Her passing shots practically leave you standing in place. She reads your footwork, weight, and center of gravity and knows exactly what type of shot to use every time.

Why does she need a coach? She needs a coach because she is not satisfied with her level of play. She wants more. She wants to tap into the talent that she already has and raise her game to a new level. Many professionals want to do the same thing in their careers.

I once worked with a financial planner and stockbroker who was already one of the top brokers in the United States, yet he was not satisfied with his life. He didn't want to be "married" to his business; rather, he wanted to begin to focus on greatness and to appreciate his family more fully. He realized that on his own he was having difficulty creating balance in his health, business, and personal life.

Jeff Verdon, a Newport Beach, California attorney, says that his weekly coaching sessions have taught him that planning, goal setting and keeping commitments are not as intimidating as he believed they would be. He has gained such clarity and focus from his coaching sessions that he has increased billings in his firm more than fifty percent. He has done this without the personal stress formerly associated with his career.

Sharon Keating, a ReMax owner, says that her coaching experience forces her to make and keep commitments to herself. The coaching has greatly helped her to identify and maintain her focus.

Bruce Wright, owner of Strategic Alliance Management & Marketing, Inc., is so convinced that having a coach will make a profound difference in his clients' performances that he has hired me to be the coach of each individual that enters into an agreement with him for his company's marketing services.

If you are a sales manager, business owner or entrepreneur whose income is influenced by the efforts of others—or if you are simply a highly motivated individual who wants the best for yourself and your family—then coaching is for you.

What is Coaching?

"Coaching is an ongoing relationship which focuses on the client taking action toward the realization of their vision, goals or desires. Coaching uses a process of inquiry and personal discovery to build the client's level of awareness and responsibility, and it provides the client with structure, support and feedback." (Professional & Personal Coaches Association *Being In Action* newsletter issue #1).

Coaching, as defined by THE COACHES Training Institute, "is a powerful alliance designed to forward and enhance the lifelong process of human learning, effectiveness and fulfillment."

My definition of coaching is an ongoing relationship with a motivated individual who is committed to improving constantly in their health, business and personal life. As a coach I am committed to the success of the person I am coaching.

Picture this: Hold your arm straight out in front of you and make a fist. The fist represents your vision, mission, goals, etc. This is where you want to be and the arm represents the direct path to your vision.

Now, my job as a coach is to help you to see when you are off the path. When are your actions not in alignment with your stated goals? This is called "holding the focus."

I will refer to the other person you are coaching as a "client" even though he or she may be a friend or co-worker and not paying for your help. In fact, this book is not designed to teach you to be a professional coach or to open a practice in coaching. For that I refer people to THE COACHES Training Institute. (Contact Laura Whitworth at 415-451-6000.) This book is designed for the individual who desires to help another person, co-worker, friend or associate with focus and performance.

Who needs coaching? Coaching is for the individual who is excited, motivated, talented, and ready to move on. Who offers coaching? A person who offers coaching is giving a gift of a lifetime. A person who offers coaching is a person who cares about you and your life. The results will be immediate and long lasting. Breakthroughs will occur in all areas of your life.

Are you excited about coaching? Then, let's begin! What are we waiting for?

CHAPTER ONE

A Definition of High Achievement

What does it mean to be a high achiever? You may recall my in-depth description in my first book, *The Sky Is Not The Limit, You Are!"* If you haven't read that book, I highly recommend that you do.

My definition of high achievement embraces several principles. Before you consider the definition, I request that you get in the right frame of mind. Forget about the American practice of evaluation by ranking. Stop thinking about comparing yourself to someone else. Ranking is not relevant. What I am interested in is how you are doing compared to yourself, that is, how you are capable of doing and how you want to be doing.

With that thought in mind, here is my definition of high achieve-ment. I would call you a high achiever if you meet this criterion:

Regardless of how high or how low your commitment level is,
you are a high achiever if you do what you say you will do
and get the maximum returns from your efforts.

At a function I attended recently as the keynote speaker, the organization brought on stage the number one producer for the company. This person was a sixteen million dollar producer while the average production for their industry was at the one million dollar level. Everyone applauded and praised this person.

My response was quite different. Simply because this person produced sixteen million does not automatically mean he was performing at an elite level. Perhaps this person worked eighteen-hour days, had no personal life, and suffered from poor health. I would not call such a person an elite performer. Would you?

The fact that this person did more than anyone else is not relevant. I would ask: did this person do what he said he would do? Did he get max-imum results from his efforts? If the answers to those questions are "yes," then I would celebrate his results.

Likewise, I would praise the part-time, single parent who did three million if her goal was three million, and she did what she said she would do.

What a wonderful world we would all live in if everyone subscribed to core value #1:

Core Value #1
I hold it important that I do what I say I will do.

This is my first value for the coaching relationship. Before I begin coaching any client, I ask for his or her agreement to this value. I ask clients to be very careful about what they commit to do because I will hold them accountable to honor this core value.

Getting agreement on another value prior to beginning the coaching relationship is essential. I will explain core value #2 with an exercise that is simple to do. Get a blank piece of paper, look at the second hand of your watch and give yourself thirty seconds to write down as many green vegetables as you can think of. Ask another person to do the same. After both of you have had thirty seconds to think of green vegetables, next, give yourself another thirty seconds but this time work as a team and compare your lists, brainstorm together, and come up with one list.

Usually, two people working together on this exercise will outperform an individual working alone. This is a concept in synergy, leading to the second core value that supports this book on coaching.

Core Value #2
I can't do it alone. I am far greater as a team than I can ever be by myself.

I must get agreement to this second core value before I will work with a client. If clients will not agree to these two core values, then they are not receptive to coaching, and I will not work with them.

Every week a part of the coaching call is going to involve accountability. Every week the clients will be asked if they did what they said they would do the previous week. If they didn't, then we will look at two areas. First, if life got in the way, we will look for options to handle life's challenges and still fulfill the commitment.

The second area we will consider is the reality of the commitment. Was it too big? Was it unrealistic? Perhaps the client's priorities changed and the commitment was no longer important to them. Regardless of the reason, it gives us significant information to consider.

CHAPTER TWO

Why Is Coaching Necessary?

The answer is quite simple. Human nature makes coaching necessary. Human beings must be able to recognize what can hurt them and to avoid those actions or situations automatically. This is true for all forms of life. Place a plant next to a window. Over time, the leaves will start to grow toward the sunlight coming in through the window since the plant is a living organism. As a living organism, it has an instinct that avoids pain and seeks comfort. In this example, the plant is seeking the comfort and life-giving resource of sunlight.

If we were to take the same plants and pipe in rock–and–roll music, there would also be a reaction to the principle of avoiding pain and seeking comfort. The plants would actually grow away from the sound because the music acts as an irritant.

Another classic experiment is known as "the rat in a box." The researcher places a hungry rat in the center of a cage or box. To the left is a long corridor. Soft rags are placed at the end of the corridor. To the right is another long corridor with food at the end of it.

When the gates to the corridors are opened, the rat immediately runs to the food. Psychologists call this "desire-driven behavior." In the absence of any obstacles, the organism (rat) will be motivated or driven by its desire (for food). When an organism is driven by its desire, an action will always be taken in an attempt to satisfy the desire. In this case, the rat will take the necessary action of running down the corridor to the right side to receive the food.

Psychologists tell us that when there are no obstacles, an organism will always be desire driven and, therefore, will take the necessary action to reach its goals.

This is a fine theory. However, I doubt that you or anyone else is living a life free of obstacles. Let's make this model more realistic and test the rat again. We put the rat back into the center of the box. We still have a motivated, hungry rat. Now, we line the floor on the right side with a metal grid. Next, we run a current across the metal grid and open the gates, giving the rat access to either the left side which contains the rags, or the right side which contains the food.

Since the rat is still driven by its desire, it will start to run over the metal grid to get food. The moment it steps on the metal grid, it gets a tremendous shock and instinctively runs to the soft, comfortable rags on the left side. The rat is doing exactly what it should be doing. It is avoiding pain and seeking comfort. This is referred to as the survival mechanism, an instinct in all of life. The survival mechanism has the function of protecting the rat. In order to protect the rat from life-threatening pain, it must be an override system. What does it override? It overrides the rat's desire or motivation to eat the food. The rat instinctively knows that it can go for months without eating and still survive, but it must avoid life-threatening pain right now.

One more principle must operate to protect the rat. This principle is to compel the rat to avoid the threat.

Survival Mechanism
1. Is an override system.
2. Compels the organism to avoid.

Since the rat is highly motivated due to its hunger, the survival instinct must immediately recognize pain and then override other motivations and compel the rat to avoid taking any dangerous action.

Here is the test: Place the rat back in the center of the box, remove the shock from the metal grid, but leave the metal grid. Will the rat take the action necessary to reach its goal? The answer is no. Why not? Because of the survival instinct. The rat previously has associated great pain with running over this metal grid.

This illustrates the weakness of the survival instinct. The survival mechanism cannot differentiate between real and false circumstances. The truth in this example is that nothing is stopping the rat from reaching its goal. However, since the rat perceives that the shock is still there and associates the activity of running over this grid with great pain, avoidance occurs.

What does that tell you about the nature of truth?

Objective truth is not relevant.
Your perception becomes your truth and your reality!

We can find many examples of this model in everyday life. The sales person who subconsciously has linked prospecting calls with rejection avoids making the calls. The overweight person who is committed to losing weight through dieting and exercising avoids both because of the association of dieting and exercising with pain. This happens every day.

Something else occurs when we are avoiding uncomfortable activities. Our brain uses a defense mechanism called rationalization to protect us. Let me explain rationalization to you by asking you three confrontational questions.

1. Would you agree that you know what you need to do right now to be more successful than you currently are?

If you are new in a particular business, change the question to a statement: "You know what you need to do to gain the knowledge necessary to be successful."

2. Would you agree that not only do you know what to do but also that you are capable of doing what you need to do to be more successful than you currently are?

3. And finally, would you agree that not only do you know what to do and how to do it, and that you are not doing everything that you could be doing to be as successful as you could possibly be in your health, business and personal life?

You probably answered "yes" to all three questions. However, I must use a coaching technique here called "**tell the truth.**" It is not likely that you are really seeing yourself in this way. If you were walking around feeling inadequate about your performances, you would get depressed, reducing your white blood cell count and leading yourself to illness.

Our brain's design is for survival. When you and I are avoiding uncomfortable activities, we don't recognize our avoidance. Instead, we go into what is called "selective perception." Selective perception means that we don't see all there is to see in our world. Our brains can only perceive certain amounts of information. For example, we don't hear certain sounds or perceive certain smells. Our senses are very limited. If you look at what appears to be the smoothest glass, held under a powerful electron microscope it is anything but smooth. The ends are jagged and uneven. However, with our limited perception, all we can sense is the edge being smooth.

Do you remember the movie *Phenomenon* with John Travolta? In that film something happens to Travolta that heightens his ability to read, think, feel, etc. He can see the energy fields of a pencil and interacts with it to move the pencil without touching it. I remember a line from the movie. Travolta is being interviewed, and when he moves the pencil he says, "We are made of the same thing." The interviewer says, "wood?" Travolta laughs and says, "No, energy." In that movie Travolta could perceive beyond the limitations of most people.

When you and I are "avoiding," we don't perceive opportunities to take action and do the activities that we have associated with pain. Instead, what we see are our reasons, stories, excuses, obstacles, priorities, etc. Then, we justify our avoidance with rationalization. This keeps us from feeling guilty for not doing what we said we would do.

I call this inner dialogue the *alien*. This refers to the internal chatter that we all have. What drives this internal chatter? The alien is driven by our instincts. The survival instinct is designed so that we orient ourselves to see only the reasons why we can't do an activity instead of the opportunities to take an uncomfortable action.

One role for the coach is to point out when the alien is doing the thinking. Just as you found more green vegetables working with someone else, a coach is able to point out what you cannot see on your own, your **alien!** This fear-based, untrue conversation is our biggest hindrance.

The purpose of rationalization by the alien is to protect you. It protects you from feeling guilty about not doing what you said you would do. The alien is a justification of avoidance. Unfortunately, such avoidance is fear based and unnecessary for your protection: it simply holds you back.

One more aspect of human nature must be added to what I call the competition for performance: our **fear** and **resistance to change.** Here is the paradox. Making more money is desirable. Losing weight is desirable. Having a great loving relationship is desirable. We all want those results. However, having those results requires us to be different from what we are. Here are the three common human types of resistance shared by all people:

1. **Resistance to do activities that we don't feel like doing.**
2. **Resistance to do activities that we perceive as being uncomfortable.**
3. **Resistance and fear of change.**

You wouldn't think that you and I would resist doing activities because we fear change. But it is a real resistance and natural human instinct. Medicine has recognized this for ages. For example, what is the natural instinct of the body when the individual receives a liver transplant? The response is to reject the foreign tissue. Doctors must use an intervention to **compensate** for the body's natural response to such change.

The same is true for you and me. When we have goals that represent being different, our natural response is to avoid that change. We also need an intervention so we don't sabotage ourselves. That intervention is coaching.

Many people don't realize they are not committed to the result. What they are committed to is the struggle. Being in "the struggle to have" lies within their comfort zone and is nonthreatening. When they get close to actually having, they are forced outside the limits of their comfort. The alien freaks out. Sabotage, followed by rationalizations, occurs. Common examples of this include: overeating, not making phone calls or following up on hot prospects, losing the phone number of a person you are interested in dating, etc.

Are you ready for some good news? It doesn't matter if you are committed to the end result or to the struggle. If you can identify what activities you will do to have what you want, if you can then identify what actions you are willing to take over the next seven days, and if you have a coach holding you accountable, then you will break through any commitments to the struggle. You don't even have to be aware that you might be committed to the struggle. Just be focused and accountable over a short period of time and away you go.

You might find, however, that you were not committed to the result you thought you wanted. From time to time, we all live lies we are not aware of. How can you discover if you are living a lie?

Committing to an activity and then consistently not doing it is a sure clue that you are living a lie.

It takes a caring and tough person to be a coach. I congratulate and applaud you for buying this book, reading it, and applying these techniques to help other people. Have you ever heard the phrase that you can get by giving? You will be giving the gifts of clarity, focus, and accountability when you are coaching another person. You will touch their lives in many ways and on many levels. Please don't wait until you are good and "have it down" to start coaching. There is no such thing as a bad coach! The fact that you are asking clients to look at their lives will be beneficial to them. You can immediately apply the techniques included in the remainder of this book and use them to make significant differences in other people's lives. So, let's look at the essential elements of coaching.

NOTES

CHAPTER THREE

The Eighteen Essential Elements of Coaching

Imagine that you are my coach. I would like to discuss the following situation with you. I have been hired by a regional real estate franchise to be their keynote speaker at a local meeting. The meeting is on Thursday morning, and I will be speaking for 90 minutes. I plan on packing for the meeting at about 4:30 p.m. on Wednesday and then going to the gym for a couple of hours. By that time rush hour will have ended so I can easily drive to the program. It will take me about two hours to set up my portable display, audiocassettes and books, go through the audiovisual equipment, check slides, get my banners displayed, etc.

The regional office calls inviting me to go to dinner as their honored guest on Wednesday evening at 7:00 p.m. They would like to have me meet the top three salespeople in the region plus the regional director of training and the regional director who has hired me for the function. I don't want to go there for a few reasons. First, in order to arrive in time for dinner, I would have to start packing by 1:00 p.m. and then leave no later than 2:30 p.m. to beat the bumper-to-bumper traffic and have time to set up my room before dinner. Second, I would lose a half day in the office. Third, they are not paying me for this time, and I am at a particularly busy time of the year for my business.

In addition to these reasons, I am a very private person and would rather spend a quiet evening by myself prior to giving a talk to a large group in the morning. Also, I would have to miss my workout if I left earlier for the dinner. I don't want to go. What do you think I should do?

Stop! Do not answer that! The most natural response for most people is to give their opinion, offer advice, and solve my problem.

Essential Elements of Coaching #1 and #2

---

1. Let clients solve their own problems.
2. The question is the answer.

One of the major outcomes of coaching is that clients take responsibility for their own outcomes and for solving their own problems. Do you really help me if your response to my question is to give me your opinion? "Don't go" or "Go" does little to help me through this situation. Let's practice the first coaching element

Client's Question: "**What do you think I should do?**"
Coach's Response: *"I don't know; what do you think you should do?"*
Coaching involves helping the client find the answer to his or her own questions.
Client's Question: "**What do you think I should do to improve my business and make more money?**"
Coach's Response: *"I don't know. What do you think you should do to improve your business and make it more profitable?"*

Do you see how easy it is to use this element of coaching? You now know a technique that will help you to have an immediate impact by creating clarity for your client. Try it.

Client's Question: "**I just can't seem to find a good relationship. What do you think I should do?**"
Coach's Response: *[Your response]*

As we will see later, you can give a number of responses to these and similar questions. However, these sample illustrations point out how clients will look to you to solve their problems if you LET them. Simply repeat the question back to them.

I was in Rhode Island a few months ago. As I scanned the radio dial searching for an easy listening station or news, I came across a talk show with a psychologist taking callers. The conversation went as follows:

Caller's Question: "**My boyfriend has been having an affair with another woman. He has been lying to me about it. He is always saying that he is short on cash, yet the other day one of my friends saw him in a fancy restaurant with this woman having dinner. It was obvious that they were intimate by the way he was all over her. How do you think I should handle this?**"
Psychologist's Response: *"Dump him! Don't even look back. I've seen this before. You can't trust this type of a man and you are just setting yourself up for real trouble and heartbreak down the road. Get rid of him right now."*
Caller's response: "**Wow! But I still love him.**"
Psychologist's Reply: *"Dump him. This type of man lies, cheats and preys on*

your vulnerability. Get as far away from him as you can as fast as you can."
Caller's response: **"Thanks for your input."**

I couldn't believe that I was hearing a trained psychotherapist saying this. It makes for an exciting radio talk show, but what real value was there for the client calling in? I say, little or no value.

Don't misunderstand. As you become more experienced with coaching, your agenda will definitely play a part in your coaching. Giving advice has a place in your coaching relationship at another point. You do not help clients by solving their problems. How would you now respond to the caller asking for help? I hope that you would respond with element #2, "the question is the answer." You would ask the client, "How do think you should handle this?"

Essential Element of Coaching #3

---

3. Follow the client's agenda, not your own.

Whose agenda was it for the caller to dump her boyfriend, hers or the psychotherapist's? Of course, it was the psychotherapist's agenda.

I am going to take the role of the radio psychotherapist for this example although, as we already mentioned, coaching is not therapy.

Caller: **"My boyfriend is cheating on me, lying, etc. What do you think I should do?"**
Coach: *"I don't know. What do you think you should do?"*
Caller: **"I have no idea, that's why I'm calling in."**
Coach: *"If you did have an idea of what to do, what would you do?"*...
or confront the client with this response: *"That is not acceptable. I'm not going to let you sit by like a helpless victim who doesn't know what to do. Now, what are your options?"*

Essential Element of Coaching #4

---

4. Confront the client's alien.

I have faith in the strength of all people. I believe the caller to the radio talk show knows exactly what she needs to do, or she has the capacity to discover it for herself. My role as a coach is to ask her questions to facilitate this discovery and encourage her to confront her alien.

Essential Element of Coaching #5

5. Foster discovery through questions.

Not everyone is comfortable with confrontation. There are many more "routes" you can select to get to the same destination. Even if you are not comfortable with confrontation, you owe it to your client to ask appropriate questions and tell the truth!

Essential Element of Coaching #6

6. Tell the truth.

Don't let your client play the victim. The truth is that your client knows or can discover what to do. Clients may need some clarification from you, but they have the answers. When you have decided to coach someone, you have made a decision to be strong for that person and point out the truth.

Let's suppose for a moment that you are absolutely stuck in a situation. You have absolutely no clue as to how to respond to a person without solving the problem and giving advice. What do you do?

Essential Element of Coaching #7

7. Ask empowering questions.

The next time you are clueless, rather than saying, "I have no idea how to help you," why not respond with this question: **"What are your options?"** This is one of the most powerful questions you can ask your client. It puts the responsibility for solving the problem right back where it belongs, in the client's lap. It also honors coaching element #1, "Let clients solve their own problems."

"What do you want to do about this?" "What's next?" "What specific action do you want to take?" "What else?" These are very potent inquiries. Again, each question brings clients back to their own resources to discover their own solutions.

"What specific action do you want to take?" is a great question that does violence to the alien!

Essential Element of Coaching #8

---

8. Request specific actions.
"Who specifically?" "What specifically?"
"By when?" "How much?"

Let's apply coaching element # 8.

Client: **"I want to lose weight."**
Coach: *"How much and by when?"*
Client: **"I would like to lose twenty pounds by the end of the year."**

Note: Later you will learn about values and principle-centered focus. This would be a great spot for the coach to ask, "What would losing twenty pounds do for you?" and then hold the client's focus to that benefit.

Coach: *"How much do you want to lose this week?"*
Client: **"I'd like to lose two pounds."**
Coach: *"What do you need to do to lose two pounds this week?"*
Client: **"I need to exercise."**
Coach: *"What types of exercise will you do this week?"*
Client: **"I want to run four times this week."**

Essential Element of Coaching #9

---

9. Coach for reality using MLO's.

I can't overemphasize the importance of element #9. Many Americans have bought into the myth that *you should commit to a high goal and then if you fall short you are better off than if you committed to a lower goal.* This is not true! Committing to high and unrealistic goals does not pull someone to a higher level of performance. If anything, committing to unrealistic goals will diminish performance. If people commit too high, then as soon as they see they can't possibly reach their goals, they will stop taking any action. Thinking is likely to be "why try?" for they've already failed.

(This will be a contested point among coaches. Many coaches will say, "Want twice as much as your client, for your client." I am looking at building momentum-creating action. At some point clients may appreciate your wanting twice as much for them but not at the beginning of a coaching relationship.)

The better approach is to use MLO's, Minimum Level Objectives. "Tell me the minimum level that I can expect you to do. You can always do more, but doing less is not acceptable."

I always try to confront unrealistic commitments because I realize the lies that are embedded there. I'm not saying that people lie on purpose. It's just that they don't know. They are not aware of what they are committing to. Their commitment looks and sounds good, so they think, "Let's do it." Approaching life like that leads to disappointment and resignation. People will begin to believe they can't succeed.

In our example, I will challenge the client on the feasibility of running four times this week with a question:

Coach: *"How long has it been since you ran four times in one week?"*
Client: **"I haven't run in about two years because I've been having problems with my knees."**

What is the chance this client will run at all? I say, very slim. A person doesn't naturally understand what it means to *make a realistic commitment*. A person is not used to making commitments and following through on them. This is what the accountability aspect does. For the first time in many individuals' lives, coaches are asking them to make commitments and be accountable for them. This results in action and accomplishments.

Essential Element of Coaching #10

---

10. Coach for accountability.

When a dramatic change takes place, the client knows you are going to ask them if they did what they said they would do. At first this might appear threatening. This issue of accountability is one reason why coaching is not for everyone. A person in a coaching program gets things done. Actions, not excuses, occur. Accountability is a gift–not an enemy!

In my live training programs, I ask the group to take out a business card and write down a specific commitment they want to accomplish over the next seven days in their health, business or personal life. Then, I take someone's card and read it to the group. I role play, and coach them for the points I have made so far regarding the essential elements of coaching. Are they specific? measurable? realistic? etc.

Next, I give them a sense of realistic accountability. Let's say the commitment is to have a business proposal finished in seven days. I would coach for more specifics on "what it means to have a finished business proposal." I would ask these questions: "What am I holding you accountable to do?" "What is measurable here?" "What are the action steps you commit to take that will lead you to finishing this proposal?" "At the end of seven days, describe to me what you have as the finished product." "What steps have you committed to take to get there?"

Once I am satisfied this commitment passes all of the *Essential Elements of Coaching* guidelines, I will lower the boom with accountability by asking: "Would you pay me $100.00 if you don't get this done in seven days?"

Many times, a person will squirm at this question. If they squirm, either they are not really committed to getting it done, or the commitment is not realistic. I need to coach it to reality. "What part of this commitment would you forfeit the $100.00 for if you don't perform?" If people are uncomfortable about committing $100.00 to me for not doing what they say they will do, where is their attention? Their attention is on the reasons why they might not get it done. They are forecasting that they can't do it, thereby setting up their reality that they won't take action.

People are used to making empty commitments and never taking action. For most people, it doesn't matter. They simply continue going on as usual. A person in a coaching program isn't allowed that option. Someone who is satisfied to simply "go on as usual" will not pay to be in a coaching program nor will they seek to be in a nonpaid coaching relationship. They simply don't want the confrontation about their performance. They qualify themselves out of the system.

Every so often, I will get an individual whose company is paying for him or her to be in the coaching program. If this person is not committed to move on in life, I will fire that person. If clients miss their calls to me, or consistently do not do what they say they will do, they will be gone from my coaching program.

I will give everyone the benefit of the doubt. I will bend over backwards to help an individual who is seeking to be better. However, I draw the line with someone who has no interest in improvement. I don't judge that person. It is perfectly fine with me that they are not motivated to excel. However, coaching is reserved for those who are motivated, and that motivation comes from within the client.

What do you do when you are stuck in your coaching and don't know where to go? Use three magic words from element #11, "Tell me more."

Essential Element of Coaching #11

---

11. Create a space for discovery using the words—Tell me more.

Let's continue with our coaching call and add in the essential elements of coaching as appropriate. (We left off with the client wanting to lose two pounds this week.) Our discussion concerned his commitment to run four times this week. We challenged him by asking when he last ran four times in a week. His response was that due to knee problems it had been years.

I still want to find out if running is a realistic option as an action for losing two pounds this week. How will I find this out? I will ask the client.

Coach: *"Is running a realistic option as an action towards losing two pounds this week? Tell me more about your knees."*

Client: **"My knees are okay even though I don't have any cartilage in my right knee. I can still run but I have to keep the pace and pounding to a minimum."**

Clients lie unintentionally and they don't know it. I want to check out wishful thinking (lies) here. I am going to use the skills of element #'s 4 and 6, *confrontation and telling the truth.*

Coach: *"How do you know that you can still run? When is the last time you ran?"*

Client: **"I was in Washington, D.C., last week for a business meeting. I ran about four miles by the White House and felt great."**

Coach: *"It sounds like you can start running again as long as you keep the pace slow."*

Client: **"That's right!"**

Coach: *"So you haven't run in two years other than last week in D. C?"*

Client: **"Right."**

Coach: *"Then, how would you feel if you only ran three instead of four*

times this week? Would that be good enough for your weight control?"
Client: **"Yeah, three times would be great!"**

I see this all the time! This client wants me to accept a commitment to run four times yet he feels great about running three times. With this attitude, it is not likely he will run four times. I am not doing him a service to accept weak commitments. After all, remember, I want him to honor his word. I want him to be one hundred percent this week and do everything that he said he would do. As his coach, I want to help him have the clarity to find out what he is really willing to do.

Coach: *"If you ran two times this week would that be enough?"*
Client: **"No, I really want to run three times."**
Coach: *"Great, that's the commitment."*

Now, what questions would you ask? What does it mean to run three times? What is missing? How about, how far? How long? When specifically? etc.

Coach: *"How long or how far will you run?"*
Client: **"There is a loop around my house that is four miles long. I will run there and, if I get tired, I will combine a run/walk."**
Coach: *"When will you do this? Are there any particular times that you want to be held accountable to run? Or is it just important that you run three times for four miles each this week?"*
Client: **"I have several times that I can run. I'll just say that I'll commit to running three times this week whenever it gets done."**

I am always thinking of element #8—who, what, when, where, how much, etc. The client's commitment may not sound like a good one, but I want to coach for flexibility.

Essential Element of Coaching #12

---

12. Coach for flexibility.

I want the client to have the chance to be one hundred percent every week. I also know there will be unscheduled interruptions, priorities, crises, etc. on a daily basis. I would rather commit the client to the *sum* of their actions rather than to specific times. In the example above, I would rather commit the client to running three times for four miles than running on Monday, Wednesday, and Friday. Running on those days might not be important to the client. If I force the commitment and something comes up and the client doesn't run on Friday, then the client has lost. What is really important is running a third day rather than running on Friday.

The way to coach for flexibility is to have the client always looking at "what if's." What would stop them? Focus on MLO's. This allows for all of the unscheduled priorities to occur, get handled and still have clients do what they say they will do, making strong efforts to finish their commitments for the week. Continuing with this same issue and same client:

Coach: *"What else do you need to do to lose two pounds this week?"*
Client: **"I need to diet."**
Coach: *"What specifically does that mean? Tell me more."*
Client: **"Well I need to reduce my intake of fat grams, eat fruits and vegetables, etc."**

I need to go through the same process taking the client from the vague to the specific and measurable. Perhaps the client agrees to count calories five out of seven days (remaining realistic and flexible). Gaining commitment to a certain amount of servings of fruits or salads, etc., we want to help the client measure progress over the next seven days.

Essential Element of Coaching #13

---

13. Coach for balance.

As a coach I am constantly holding the focus for the client. Most clients tell me that they want to be more successful and make more money. I probe further with, "Tell me more." The client usually continues with what having money will give them, i.e., security, safety, peace of mind, etc. Whether clients know it or not, in order to make money, provide for their families and improve their relationships with their spouses, they need to be healthy.

In the capacity of coach, I always coach for balance and keep clients looking for ways to improve. Many times they are in a rut in their business and think the solution exists in their business. In fact, the solution to improving their business might be in some other area such as a relationship with a spouse or a child, or their health.

A good friend of mine, Ed Laird, is 54 years old and facing triple bypass surgery. Ed doesn't want to have this intrusive surgery and knows there are options. The most viable option is to lose fifty pounds, but he doesn't think he can do it. This is an opportunity for me as his friend and as a coach to practice element #14.

Essential Element of Coaching #14

---

14. Stretch your clients.

Ed is an example of, "coach for balance," but he also serves as an example for "stretch your clients" because he doesn't think that he can lose fifty pounds.

As I work with Ed, my objective is to change his point of view. I know he can lose weight if he keeps weight loss in perspective. Suppose Ed visits overseas and flies from Saudi Arabia to Israel, then to London, and on to New York for business. Just imagine that his plane is hijacked in Israel and the hijackers see his American passport. They rush him off the plane, blindfolded, and take him as a hostage.

For Ed's safety, they move him every day. They move him through back alleys and always on foot. Every day Ed is jogging about five miles at a very slow pace but five miles nonetheless. They only feed him small portions of rice, water, bread and some scraps of poultry.

This goes on for several weeks. Do you think that Ed is going to lose weight? The answer is, *"of course."* Now, let's reproduce this sense of urgency, priority, and commitment without the crisis. The desire to lose weight has to come from Ed. The fact that he has a major health challenge probably is not going to be a factor. Ed has known for a long time that he needed to lose weight. What has to happen?

Ed needs a coach. He needs to be guided in confronting his fears, the alien. He needs to develop daily habits, be held accountable to specific activities, and change his thinking and his lifestyle. How does he change his thinking? One way is to make a tape with Baroque music and put statements on tape that represent the type of thinking he will need to support his new lifestyle. He has already done this. Now he needs to listen to it in his car for five minutes everyday. We can assume this is internal support.

Next, he needs to take it one day and one week at a time. I will use all of the elements of coaching that I have talked about so far to help Ed specifically identify what his challenges are and what activities he needs to accomplish to reach his goals.

I will not be his long-term coach. Our friendship doesn't allow me to be the objective third party required of a coach. I can't be his coach because I am too attached to the outcome, so I will begin the coaching and then refer him to another trained coach.

My challenge in Ed's case is to have him surrender in his business and place full attention on his health. Ed must realize that he can actually get more done in business by easing back on "business time" and spending that "saved time" on his health. His relationships with his spouse, children, and friends are strong so the real shift is health.

The world we live in today is very complex, full of transition, paradox and chaos. Once the support structure of the coaching relationship is in place, clients have a *safe space* to begin focusing on the principles of balance, fulfillment and the process of their lives rather than rushing to put out fires.

Balance is dynamic, not static. Balance is ever changing. Try balancing on one foot. You will notice that perfect balance is a fleeting moment. For the most part, you are constantly making adjustments, sometimes minor and sometimes major, to maintain "balance."

The essence of balance is *discrimination,* or the ability to choose. Balance is the capacity to say, "Yes, I will include this in my life," or "No, I will let go of this. I will exclude this from my life." As our world grows more complex, this ability to discriminate becomes increasingly important if we are to maintain a sense of balance and harmony in our lives. We must be able to say "no" and to let go of, exclude or cut away those things that do not serve us. This implies that we are able to prioritize (determine that which is most valuable to us) and that we are willing to let go of the things that are at the lower end of the scale.

Unfortunately, we often want to have it all. Given the ever-increasing range of opportunities available to us, we become like children, gobbling too much Halloween candy and then suffering from a terrible stomach ache. We must be able to choose powerfully and clearly what the components of our lives will be. Otherwise, we will miss the magnificent moments of our lives while struggling to keep too many balls in the air.

Choice and surrender are *proactive* as opposed to *reactive*: they imply responsibility. You are taking charge of your life and choosing the life *you* want, instead of letting circumstances in your life choose for you. While this level of personal responsibility is often challenging, it makes the difference between having a life you can celebrate, or tolerating whatever circumstances get dumped on you.

For example, I had to make a choice in order to write this book. I have wanted to write these pages for a long time but the project was a "one-of-these-days" priority. The alien had me, for my alien's conversation convinced me that I was too busy marketing my business and coaching practice to take the time to write this book.

What a lie! The alien is always a liar. In truth, I was afraid to let go of my personal marketing: I was afraid to surrender. I disguised this fear as a positive trait and applauded myself for working so hard in my business. I work with speakers' bureaus and have a full-time marketing director but my rationalization was that there is so much opportunity out there that I didn't want to lose any time. I've got to be on the phone.

So, what was happening? I was making 150–200 calls per week. I was making progress in booking myself. But I was stuck working in my business as opposed to working <u>on</u> my business. I needed to say "no" to prospecting or "no" to writing a book. Therefore, I needed to make a decision. As a result, I decided to take three weeks off from marketing and work full time on the book. The world will not stop if Bob Davies stays off the phone for three weeks. With a little earlier start in the morning when I get back on the phone, I will be caught up in my marketing in no time and I will have a book.

The same process was going on in another area of my life. I am a private pilot. It is dangerous and inconvenient to have no instrument rating and to be unable to fly in conditions of limited visibility. I've failed to set aside time in advanced instrument training. I once took off from John Wayne airport on a beautiful, sunny afternoon for a trip to Big Bear Lake. When I called for weather information prior to my return, I learned that the John Wayne airport was reporting a marine layer had moved in and the airport was overcast. I couldn't fly in without an instrument rating.

What was the answer? **Surrender!** The instrument rating is project number two for this year. I will set aside time to get my rating. Then I will come back, get caught up in business with a new book and an instrument rating! How about that?!

A very good question to ask clients is, "Where do you need to say 'no,'" and "where do you need to say 'yes?'" Letting go and taking a step back to spring forward works. As I surrender to do these projects, I will still be focusing on my priorities of health and relationships.

Essential Element of Coaching #15

15. Coach for fulfillment.

Fulfillment occurs when people are "on purpose" and fully honor their primary values. The focus of our culture is acquiring, having, and achieving. Most people think if they have what they want, they will be happy. They focus on having the right job, the perfect relationship, the best toys, achieving the gold medal, the next rung on the ladder, or status on the job. The satisfaction from focusing on those elements is short lived and seems to leave an emptiness or profound sense of dissatisfaction with life. Desperation escalates as people rush down the tunnel called "having = fulfillment" and find having ≠ fulfillment.

People want to be happy, secure, and fulfilled. Focusing on "having" will not lead to this. The coach's job is to accompany the client in gaining clarity about what *real* fulfillment is for them. The coach focuses the client's attention on what will truly fulfill them rather than on "having" and "acquiring." This shifting of perspective is one of the fundamental principles of coaching.

We will work on this area as we get into the intake portion of this book. Where you want to coach from is the philosophy that fulfillment occurs in the realm of "being" rather than in the realm of "having."

Essential Element of Coaching #16

16. Coach for process.

Most of us spend the majority of *our* time being concerned about results and goals in our lives. In so doing, we actually miss our lives. Happiness and satisfaction do not necessarily occur after results. Fulfillment occurs when a person is happy in the *process* of life. *Process* is a state of being; result is in the domain of having.

When our lives are filled with "being" instead of "having," we have richer, fuller lives. A coach can be drawn into the "results trap." Our responsibility as coaches is to remind the client frequently, especially at the outset of the relationship, that we are interested in working with the process of life, as well as results. A coach is more than simply an accountability machine.

The most common way for the client to understand this distinction is to closely examine daily habits and disciplines. Instead of always relating actions to a projected result, track the satisfaction that comes from those actions. Ask the following questions when a goal or projected result is expressed: "Are you committed to the day-to-day process involved in the accomplishment of that result? Will the process itself be satisfying, regardless of the outcome?"

The client must also be in action. I am not talking about *process* at the expense of action. Some clients will love any excuse not to be in action. They simply love to chat about their process ad infinitum. Months later you will notice that nothing has changed in the quality of their lives.

When clients focus their attention on *process* rather than results, they will notice less stress in their lives; consequently, they produce more results. Another good question to ask your client is: "Who do you need to become to reach this goal?"

Essential Element of Coaching #17

---

17. Conclude the coaching call with an inquiry.

Inquiries are powerful questions that encourage the client to look for blind spots and hidden areas that they would not likely see by themselves. An inquiry such as, "What are you tolerating?" can stimulate tremendous insight for the client. Use inquiries in your coaching call on a frequent basis. We will discuss inquiries more fully in the next chapter on intake principles.

Essential Element of Coaching #18

---

18. Champion the client.

Offer generous support, encouragement, and reinforcement to clients. Let them know frequently how much you believe in them. Let them know who they have become, and what they have accomplished over time. If you don't believe in a client, refer that client to another coach.

The Eighteen Essential Elements of Coaching

1. Let clients solve their own problems.
2. The question is the answer.
3. Follow the client's agenda, not your own.
4. Confront the client's alien.
5. Foster discovery through questions.
6. Tell the truth.
7. Ask empowering questions.
8. Ask for specific actions: who, what, by when, where, how much?
9. Coach for reality using MLO's.
10. Coach for accountability.
11. Create a space for discovery using the words: "Tell me more."
12. Coach for flexibility.
13. Coach for balance.
14. Stretch your clients.
15. Coach for fulfillment.
16. Coach for process.
17. Leave the coaching call with an inquiry.
18. Champion the client.

CHAPTER FOUR

The Intake

How do you prepare your client for the first coaching call? Twenty coaches are likely to have twenty different responses to this question. The first call allows us to obtain necessary information and begin our coaching relationship.

There really isn't a right or wrong way to go with the intake. Simply blend your personality, intuition, and basic coaching techniques into your coaching.

The following pages of this book contain forms I use for a client intake:

❏ Form #1: Coaching cover page. (pg. 30)

❏ Form #2: Confidential coaching data form. (pgs. 31–35)

❏ Form #3: Commitment sheets. (pgs. 131–132)

❏ Form #4: Values clarification sheets. (pgs. 40–41)

❏ Form #5: Categories wheel. (pg. 48)

❏ Form #6: Weekly planning calendar. (pg. 54)

❏ Form #7: Articles on coaching. (appendix 133–140)

The coaching cover page is self-explanatory.

The coaching data form is helpful as a first document to gather information. As you can see, personal data such as name, birthdate, company, business, home phone and fax numbers, partner name, children's names and ages, special dates, etc. are all helpful information. When I speak to a client, I have this information in front of me. Let clients know you care about all parts of their lives and not just their production. Asking about their children, partner, mother-in-law, etc. will show them that you care.

Coaching

A powerful alliance designed to forward and enhance the lifelong process of human learning, effectiveness, and fulfillment.

High Performance Training, Inc.
Bob Davies, President
Coaching Data Form — CONFIDENTIAL

Name: _____

Birthdate: _____

Company: _____

Title/Position: _____

Business Phone: _____

Business Fax: _____

Home Phone: _____

Home Fax: _____

Number of years with current company: _____

In current profession: _____

Marital Status: _____

Number of children: _____

Partner/Companion Information

Name: _____

Birthdate: _____

Wedding or special anniversary date: _____

Name(s) of child(ren) and age(s): _____

_____

_____

_____

As a coach, I need to understand how you view the world in general and yourself in particular. Each person comes from a unique place in his or her thinking and in the way he or she interacts with those around them.

Our confidentiality and trust begin now. Answer each of the following questions as clearly and thoughtfully as possible, expressing the best of who you are. These are "pondering" type questions designed to stimulate your thinking in a particular way which will make our work together more productive. I suggest that you take several days to compose your responses to the following questions. Thank you.

Business:

Why did you choose your current profession?

_____

_____

_____

_____

What do you like most about the work that you do?

_____

_____

_____

_____

What do you like least?   _____

_____

_____

_____

As a professional, in which areas do you consider yourself to be most effective?   _____

_____

_____

_____

In which areas would you like to see yourself improve or change?

_____

_____

_____

_____

If you could wave a magic wand and create the perfect situation for yourself as a professional and as a person, what would that look like?   _____

_____

_____

_____

Health:

How would you rate your commitment to your health at this time? (0 to 10)_____

Has it ever been higher or lower? Explain._____

_____

_____

What do you want me to know about your overall physical health?

_____

_____

_____

Do you belong to a gym? Which one? _____

_____

Are you currently on an exercise program? _____

Personal:

What accomplishments or measurable events must, in your opinion, occur during your lifetime so that you will consider your life to have been satisfying and well lived, a life of few or no regrets? _____

_____

_____

_____

If you had a secret passion in your life, something which is almost too exciting to actually do or do more of, what would it be? ____

_____

_____

_____

What do you consider your role to be in your local community, the United States, and the world? _____
_____
_____
_____

If you could devote your life to contributing to or serving others, and still have the money and lifestyle you needed, would you do it? _____
_____
_____

If yes, how would it look? _____
_____
_____

What tips would you give me to tell me how you are best managed? _____
_____
_____

If you had a 5-year goal and you had the continuing services of a coach to help you make it happen and money was not an issue, what would that goal be? What difference would working with a coach make? _____
_____
_____

What is missing in your life that would make your life more fulfilling if present? _____
_____
_____

Do you believe in God or the concept of a higher power? If so, please describe the most useful and empowering aspects of your relationship with God. If not, which reference point do you use? _____
_____

Please describe your life's purpose: what it is, how it impacts your day-to-day living, how you know it's the right one for you

_____

_____

_____

What else would you like for your coach to know about you?

_____

_____

_____

I have found these questions to be particularly helpful in revealing information and clues for how to best help an individual through the coaching relationship. For example:

1. **Why did you choose your current profession?**
   As you ask this question, listen for what drives this person. What values and principles come from their answers?

2. **What do you like most about the work that you do?**

3. **What do you like least?**

4. **As a professional, in which areas do you consider yourself to be most effective?**

5. **In which areas would you like to see yourself improve or change?**
   Response allows me to coach for specific actions. When? How much? etc.

6. **If you could wave a magic wand and create the perfect situation for yourself as a professional and as a person, what would it look like?**
   This is called future pacing as it takes the client out to the future and creates a compelling vision of what is possible. I use this as a format to backtrack from the future to the present and map out a strategy to go from the present to that compelling future.

7. **How would you rate your commitment to your health at this time?** (0 to 10) I am looking for reality here. If clients rate their commitment a high number, I want to make sure their actions are in alignment with their commitments. If it is a low number, then work must be done to identify their health priority and to form a daily plan to reach the goals that we will identify.

8. **What do you want me to know about your overall health?**

9. **Do you belong to a gym? Which one?**

10. **Are you currently on an exercise program?**

11. **What accomplishments or measurable events must, in your opinion, occur during your lifetime so that you will consider your life to have been satisfying and well lived, a life of few or no regrets?** This answer will be revealing in identifying values and vision.

12. **If there were a secret passion in your life, something which is almost too exciting to do or do more of, what would it be?** This gives me information about congruency. If the client identifies some area that is a passion for them but they are not spending time in that area, I am going to want to explore that.

13. **What do you consider your role to be in your local community, the U.S., and the world?**

14. **If you could devote your life to contributing to or serving others, and still have the money and lifestyle you needed, would you do it? How would it look?**

15. **What tips would you give me on how you are best managed?** This question lets the client give me an idea of what type of coaching would work best for them.

16. **If you had a five-year goal and you had the continuing services of a coach to help you make it happen, and if money were not an issue, what would that goal be? What difference would working with a coach make?** This will help clients identify the value that they can

expect to receive from working with you.

17. **What is missing in your life, the presence of which would make your life more fulfilling?** This is a key question for you to gather clues about what really drives clients and what they really want.

18. **Do you believe in God or the concept of a higher power? If so, please describe the most useful and empowering aspects of your relationship with God. If not, which reference point do you use?**

19. **Please describe your life's purpose: what it is, how it impacts your day-to-day living, how you know it's the right one for you.**

20. **What else would you like for your coach to know about you?**
    My goal as coach is to create a values identification or clarification with the client and then form a mission statement. This serves as a principal tool to help both coach and client measure when the client is off target.

    People yearn for meaningful, rich, and significant lives. This book is about coaching clients to design their lives from the perspective of personal fulfillment—to take a stand for the quality of their lives and to discover values that fulfill and nourish them.

Values Clarification

As a coach, clarifying the client's values allows you to learn more about clients and gives clients a greater sense of who they are. If clients' goals are not in alignment with their values, they will usually struggle and suffer. Values are what pull people out of bed in the morning. Values are who you are at the moment. Honoring your values means following the age-old axiom, "Be true to yourself."

Coaches and clients need to know what values are *not*. They are not morals. Webster defines morals as principles of right and wrong in behavior. In other words, morals are capable of being used in a judgment or decision-making process. Values, on the other hand, are something "intrinsically valuable or desirable, that which belongs to the essential nature or constitution of a thing" (person, department, company). While people can make decisions about their morals, they already live their values.

Clarifying your values is not a choice or "decision-making" process. Rather, it is a discovery to uncover values which are already intrinsic to you and your life (or to your company). A delineation of personal or corporate values serves as a powerful tool in determining whether or not a given decision will be fulfilling. A review of personal, departmental or organizational values is the ultimate decision-making matrix, regardless of the outcome.

Honoring clients' values helps them escape the tyranny of the "shoulds." This is not a shopping list approach where a person chooses those values that they would *like* to have or they *should* have; instead it is a deeper look at what exists now in their lives.

We all have the same values, but we prioritize and articulate our values differently. When clients articulate their values, they deepen the meaning by attaching their own individual definitions. I have the client elaborate on what the value means to them using slash marks to separate various interpretations. For example, one way to define the value "integrity" is: "integrity/truth/honesty/walk your talk." A different, but equally valid expression of the same value is: "integrity/congruency/integrated/honesty." The articulation and the prioritization of the client's values is what makes each client unique.

Values are intangible. Therefore, if a client says money is a value, a coach helps him or her to look deeper to find the value behind the money. Look deeper to see what having money will do for the client. What value does having money fulfill? Always look beyond the tangible to the deeper source of fulfillment.

People tend to judge their values. They tend to include values they think they should have (such as spirituality and integrity), and they exclude values that society says are not acceptable (such as power and recognition). Usually our more significant values are so automatically honored that they become invisible and are often overlooked when doing values clarification. Your job as a coach is to help the client see the invisible.

How to clarify values

To begin clarifying values, the coach explains the concept of values and how the process works. Then, the coach inquires about clients' values, working with clients to expand on the phrases or words they use. If the client is at a loss, you can point to various aspects of life that will help them uncover their values.

You can either have a client clarify their values as a homework assignment or you can work with the client to do this during the coaching call. I prefer to have clients do this on their own and then discuss what they come up with. The following questions and assignments will assist them.

Statements and questions used to clarify values

1. Look at snapshots in time when life was really good. Those fond memories are times when a value was being honored.

2. Look at a time when you were particularly upset or angry. Look at feelings which caused the anger. Turn those feelings over and you will find a value that was being suppressed.

3. Look at what you must have in your life (outside of food, shelter, clothing, etc.), and you will find a value.

4. Use future self-visualization to find values. (This process will be explained after the following assignments.)

5. Attend your own 90th birthday party. What would people be saying about you? What would you want them to say about you?

Assignments

1. Make a list of 12-20 values. Use the information from the intake package to help you. Prioritize the top ten. This is just a first draft. Values show up over time, not simply in one sitting.

2. Next, evaluate how fully you are honoring those values by scoring them on a scale of zero to ten. Ask yourself what you would need to do to go to a score of ten.

Honoring values isn't easy; however, working with a coach will bring satisfaction by helping you to live authentically with yourself.

VALUES CLARIFICATION

How important are your values to you? Pick your top ten values and prioritize them. Next rank your behavior. How well do you live these values?

VALUE	IMPORTANCE	BEHAVIOR
Accomplishment/Results		
Achievement		
Adventure/Excitement		
Aesthetics/Beauty		
Altruism		
Autonomy		
Clarity		
Commitment		
Community		
Completion		
Connecting/Bonding		
Creativity		
Emotional health		
Environment		
Freedom		
Forward the Action		
Fun		
Honesty		
Humor		

VALUE	IMPORTANCE	BEHAVIOR
Integrity		
Intimacy		
Joy		
Leadership		
Loyalty		
Openness		
Personal Growth/Learning		
Mastery/Excellence		
Orderliness/Accuracy		
Nature		
Partnership		
Power		
Privacy/Solitude		
Recognition/Acknowledgement		
Risk-taking		
Romance/Magic		
Security		
Self-Expression		
Sensuality		
Service/Contribution		
Spirituality		
Trust		
Vitality		

Instructions for Future Self-Visualization

This is an excellent tool to help your client to identify values. I fax the Future Self-Visualization page directly to the client and ask a client to go through this. This will reveal many of the hidden values a client has.

The last step in the values clarification process is to have clients evaluate how fully they are honoring their top ten values by scoring them on a scale of zero to ten. Use this process throughout your coaching relationship as a diagnostic tool. Ask clients what they would need to do to have their scores be a ten.

Get into a comfortable position, either sitting in your chair or lying on the floor. Next, close your eyes and take three deep breaths. As you inhale, tell your body to relax; on the exhale, allow the tension to flow out. You might want to start at the top of your head or the soles of your feet and have relaxation conversation with the different areas of your body, asking them to relax and then feeling the relaxation as it settles into your body. ——Good—— Next, bring your attention to the spot between your eyes, the third eye. Imagine a light there.——Good—— Now imagine that light becoming a beam that extends out into space. Follow that beam as it leaves this building, as it travels above the city, as it continues out so that you can make out the entire area. Keep on going and notice the curvature of the earth.——Good ——Keep going and notice that big blue/green ball below with all the white clouds wisping around it. Enjoy this perspective for a moment.——Good—— Now notice another beam of light close to you: it may be a different color or quality. Begin to follow that beam back down to earth. This beam is taking you back to earth 20 years from now. Keep following this beam down, noticing the curvature of the earth and the geography stretched out below you. ——Good—— As you come closer to the end of the beam, keep noticing where you are. This is where your future self lives.——Good—— Come in contact with the earth and notice where you are. Notice what dwellings or nature surrounds you. ——Good—— Now, move to the dwelling of your future self. Do what you need to do to get someone to come to the door. ——Good—— On the other side of the door is your future self, your self 20 years from now; as the door opens, what do you notice? Greet your future self and notice the way your future self returns your greeting. Take in this person— this future self. Notice where he or she lives and move with him or her to a comfortable place for conversation. As you move through this place, notice the qualities and nature of the place and the person who lives there. When you arrive at the conversation place, make yourself comfortable. You might have a few questions you want to ask this person. Please ask these questions first: What is it that I most remember about the last 20 years? What do I need to be most aware of to get me from here to there? ——Good—— Now you might want to ask a few questions of your own. ——Good—— Now, one final question before you go. What other name are you called by? Thank your future self and find your way back to the beam of light and journey back up the beam, watching the world grow ever smaller as you soar out into space. ——Good—— Now, you can intersect with that beam of light that takes you back to (the current year) at (current location). ——Good—— Follow that beam back to earth noticing the area, the city and, finally, the current location. In a few moments you'll return and open your eyes. After you do, remain silent and take notes on your journey. When you are ready, open your eyes.

Mission Statements

The intake coaching call is also an opportunity for you to help your client create a mission statement. A mission statement expresses a person's purpose, vision and contribution. A mission statement is a guideline that enables you and clients to measure progress and the direction they are headed.

Since I'm a private pilot, I am fond of using an example from my flying experiences. I fly a Cessna 172. I love to fly into Santa Barbara airport from John Wayne in Southern California. I can taxi to the end of the runway, park the plane, and walk to the beach.

I have a series of navigational aids available to me as I fly from Santa Barbara back into John Wayne. I tune my navigational radio to the Santa Monica Airport at 110.80. It gives me a directional heading to follow to get to the airport, which is a checkpoint on my return to John Wayne. My equipment indicates where I am in relationship to where I am going. In the picture that follows, you can see that I have a heading of 090°. The line in the middle is off center to the left, which tells me I need to center the needle by flying 10° to the left. How else would I know where I am when all I can see are clouds?

A mission statement functions in much the same way. It tells you that you are on course, or off. It gives you a basis for evaluation and correction.

The following is my company's mission statement: We are a performance enhancement research and development company specializing in empowering individuals to personal fulfillment. We teach a system that breaks through fears into commitment, focus, and accountability. This results in measurable increased quality, service, and productivity in each person's life.

The following are some tips you can use to help your clients to form their own mission statements:

❏ 1. **What are you here for? What is your purpose?**

❏ 2. **Define what you want to be and do.**

❏ 3. **Identify an influential person.**

You can often identify what is important to you by looking to a person who has been highly influential in your life and thinking about the contribution he/she has made to your personal development. Answer the following questions, keeping in mind your personal goals for what you want to be and do. Who has been the most influential person in your life? Which of their qualities do you most admire? What qualities have you gained or do you desire to gain from that person?

❏ 4. **Identify your success image.**

To create your own success image you must know what works for you. This will help you to focus on it. You also need to identify the principles you value, the things that motivate and guide all of us. Respond to these requests:

Identify three accomplishments.

How did you do accomplish them?

What worked for you in these accomplishments?

What didn't work?

What principles are the most important to you? (honesty, trust-worthiness, love, integrity, etc.)

What one character trait would you most want to give to **all** children? What's the one thing you are not presently doing that would most improve your business?

❏ **5. Define your life roles.**

Who are you? Who are you at work, at home with your family, in the community, and in other areas of your life? These are the roles you fill. They become a natural framework to give order to what you want to do and to be. What are two or three things you would like to have happen in each area now, or in the future?

❏ **6. Project yourself in time and write a paragraph or two on how you would most like to be described in a particular role.**

By identifying your life roles, you will gain perspective and balance. By writing these descriptive statements, you will begin to visualize your highest self. You will also identify the core principles and values you desire to live.

❏ **7. Write a draft of your personal mission statement.**

Create a rough draft of your mission statement. Draw heavily upon the thinking you've done in the previous steps. In the next few weeks, carry this draft with you and make notes, additions, and deletions before you attempt another draft. Be sure it inspires the best within you. Use the following format:

I am_____

Who does _____

So that _____

❏ **8. Evaluate.**

Personal mission statements require updating. Periodic review and evaluation can help you keep in touch with your own development and keep your statement in harmony with your deepest self. Continually ask yourself the following questions:

Is my mission based on timeless, proven principles? Which ones? Do I feel that this represents the best that is within me?

During my best moments, do I feel good about what this represents? Do I feel direction, purpose, challenge, and some motivation when I review this statement?

Am I aware of the strategies and skills that will help me accomplish what I have written? What do I need to start doing now to be where I want to be tomorrow?

I ask the client to do most of the values clarification and mission statement work as homework assignments. I keep faxed copies of this information as part of our diagnostic toolkit. We make reference to it as the coaching process continues over time.

One of the things I do on the first call with the client is to go over the **Categories Wheel** on the next page with them. I ask each client to rate themselves in all areas on the wheel with two criteria:

1. Don't compare yourself to other people.
2. Rate yourself compared to where you are now and where you want to be.

I condense the wheel into three areas: business, health, and personal life. I ask the client to rate each area from zero to ten. Then I ask which area the client wants to focus on first. Sometimes I ask which area is most painful for them and which area they would rather stay away from. Often, I go to the area they wish to avoid first.

CATEGORIES

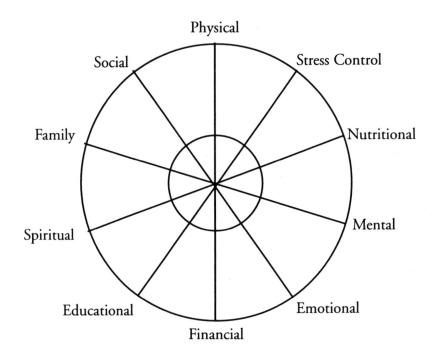

Physical –   Develop and maintain a high level of energy.
                      Consistent physical exercise. Six to seven hours
                      of sleep per night.

Stress Control –   Ability to resist illness and disease. Fear and anxi-
                      ety cause muscles to contract and blood vessels
                      to constrict. Illness sets in when blood cannot be
                      delivered freely to the body's tissues, providing
                      oxygen, nutrients, and antibodies.

Nutritional –   Habit of eating nutritious foods. Observation of
                      calories, low fat, low sodium, low refined flour,
                      and sugar diet.

Mental –	Vivid imagination of goals. Positive attitude and setting of conditions. Effective use of the limiting conscious mind. Do it now!
Emotional –	Confront and conquer fear. Change adversity to opportunity. Ability to perceive constructive feedback as positive to change. Capable of turning rejections into enthusiasm.
Financial –	Money flows. Dollar sense.
Educational –	Constantly seeking opportunities to have the academic competitive edge. Reading, tapes, etc.
Spiritual –	Direction of purpose plus energy to fulfill purpose. Sense of Higher Self.
Family –	An appreciation of those you love.
Social –	Build warm and lasting relationships.

Let's role play. John Smith's mission statement is: (I am _____.) "I am a loving and caring father and husband. I provide financial security for my family and am supportive and caring to my friends." (Who does_____.) "I am an expert financial planner and provide solutions for prosperity and security through managed money and estate planning for my clients." (So that _____.) "I am constantly committed to improvement in my health, business, and personal life. I care about all people and am a generous contributor to AIDS research."

In speaking with John, I would go into detail about what daily actions he takes to fulfill his mission statement. However, let's assume that those issues will be addressed throughout our coaching relationship. Let's begin our first coaching call.

Coach: *"I see you rate yourself as a six in your business. What does that mean?"*

Client: **"That means I need to get more of my business to be in managed accounts and I need to get more 'A' level clients."**

Coach: *"Tell me more."*

Client: "An 'A' level client is a person with over two million in manageable assets. I want to stop working smaller accounts that take up time but don't really produce much income."

Coach: *"What does it look like to go from a six to an eight in your business?"*

[The client begins to outline the specific numbers needed and the specific activities required in order to have this happen.]

Coach: *"Of all of the activities you have mentioned, have you developed a timeline for their accomplishment?"*

Client: "Well, I have an idea of when things need to be accomplished."

[This is too vague for me to accept. I will ask the client to be very specific and to tell me what the commitments are for the next seven days.One of the items that the client has mentioned he needs to do is to form a strategic alliance with an accountant and an attorney. Let's pick it up on that.]

Coach: *"Tell me more about this strategic alliance."*

Client: "One of the ways that I will get in front of high net worth people is to develop an alliance with an accountant and attorney so that we form a team to service each other's clients.

Coach: *"Great! What specifically do you need to do to form this alliance?"*

Client: "I need to do a mailing to accountants and attorneys."

Coach: *"When will you do that?"*

Client: "Well, I need to have a credibility piece prepared to include in the mail out."

Coach: *"What else do you need to have before you do a mail out?"*

Client: "I need to have something to mail them about moving from a transactional broker to a money-management, relationship-oriented broker. I want to offer full service to my clients and provide high value for them."

Coach *(holding the focus):* *"So how will you develop a strategic alliance?"*

Client: "One way to do this is to have a strategic alliance luncheon where I bring in a speaker to talk about this concept and find out who is interested."

Coach: *"Are you going to do this? When?"*

Client: "Well, I need to find out what my budget is before I make any commitments."

Hold everything! This client is scattered. I will use essential elements of coaching #4, confront the client's alien; #6, tell the truth; and #8, request specific actions.

Coach: *"Let me interrupt for a moment. I have a hunch you lack focus here. Would you agree?"*

Client: "Well, I've been so busy producing that I haven't had the time to sit down and read through my marketing plan and commit to this."

[The alien is using the excuse that he is too busy. I need to go in this direction and find out what his commitments really are. I need to find out what his future vision is and what the most productive activity is that he could be doing on a daily basis. Will working with smaller clients move him to his goal?]

Coach: *"How important is forming this strategic alliance to you?"*

Client: "Very important."

Coach: *"Okay, I have a request for you. I request that you write down everything that you need to do or have in place to put together your strategic marketing team. On our next call, I request that you have a time line prepared and be ready to tell me what you will commit to do over the next seven days. Will you do that?"*

Client: "Yes, I will. That's a great idea."

[Next I will coach for some specific actions that the client will commit to do over the next seven days in his business, health, and personal life. I will bring his attention to the weekly planner sheet that he has received in the intake package. I ask each client to be very specific with time accountability. I want each client to "predict" the next seven days. This time prediction begins with the plotting of all time commitments that the client knows about for the next seven days. I have an example for you.]

Note: Refer to sample Weekly Planner on page 53.

WEEKLY PLANNER

DATE: Mon. June 7—Sun. June 13

TIME	MON-7	TUES-8	WED-9	THUR-10	FRI-11	SAT-12	SUN-13
6:00	6:00 Wake-up Breakfast	6:00 Wake-up 6:30 Office calls	6:00 Wake-up Travel to LAX, Delta 8:45 Fly	6:00 Wake-up		Sleep in	Sleep in
7:00	7:25 Coaching call 1				7:00 Wake-up 7:30 Office calls 8:30		
8:00		8:30				8:30 Racquetball	
9:00	9:00 Coaching call 2 9:35 Coaching call 3	9:00 Gym		9:00 Program: Padgett Bus. Services	Gym 10:00		
10:00	10:05 Coaching call 4 10:45 Coaching call 5	10:30 Breakfast				10:30	
11:00	11:20 Gym	11:30 11:45 Office calls	Travel			11:30 Fly to Big Bear for Lunch Cessna 1094 F	11:00 Beach w/ Danielle
12:00	12:30 -1:30 Lunch			12:00	Office calls		
1:00	1:45 Coaching call 6						
2:00	2:30 Coaching call 7	Office calls			2:00 Paperwork		
3:00	3:05 Coaching call 8 3:45 Coaching call 9			3:50 Delta Travel	3:00 Gym		
4:00	4:30 Coaching call 10					4:00	
5:00	5:15 Coaching call 11	5:00 5:30 Gym	5:15 Arrive Memphis		5:00 Danielle	5:00 Movies w/ Danielle	
6:00	6:00 Gym						
7:00	7:00 Dinner	Pack for trip		7:51 Arrive LAX Drive to Orange County.			
8:00							
9:00							
10:00		50 Calls			40 Calls		90 Calls

WEEKLY PLANNER

Date: From _____ To _____

Time							
6:00							
7:00							
8:00							
9:00							
10:00							
11:00							
12:00							
1:00							
2:00							
3:00							
4:00							
5:00							
6:00							
7:00							
8:00							
9:00							
REMARKS							

Time accountability

Time accountability is a top priority for me and for anyone with whom I work. When a person is in control of time, tasks are completed. Time doesn't wait for anyone. Time moves ahead whether you are ready or not.

As a football coach at Cal State Fullerton, I would script two-hour thirty minute practices in five-minute intervals. I did this with my marketing director in Florida. Even though he was an independent contractor, I was paying him a guaranteed fee for his project marketing. He was free to use his time any way he wished. I insisted, however, that he be accountable for his time. It was okay for him to work for two hours on his own project that had nothing to do with my business. What was not okay was for him to be unable to account for those two hours.

My marketing person needs to be able to tell me exactly how he has spent his day, how many calls he has made, to whom, what the results were, whom he has sent information to, etc. I use the following form with him.

CALLS	TIME	CONTACTS	CALLS	TIME	CONTACTS	MONDAY 7				
						1	11	21	31	41
						2	12	22	32	42
						3	13	23	33	43
						4	14	24	34	44
						5	15	25	35	45
						6	16	26	36	46
						7	17	27	37	47
						8	18	28	38	48
						9	19	29	39	49
						10	20	30	40	50

CALLS	TIME	CONTACTS	CALLS	TIME	CONTACTS	TUESDAY 8				
						1	11	21	31	41
						2	12	22	32	42
						3	13	23	33	43
						4	14	24	34	44
						5	15	25	35	45
						6	16	26	36	46
						7	17	27	37	47
						8	18	28	38	48
						9	19	29	39	49
						10	20	30	40	50

CALLS	TIME	CONTACTS	CALLS	TIME	CONTACTS	WEDNESDAY 9				
						1	11	21	31	41
						2	12	22	32	42
						3	13	23	33	43
						4	14	24	34	44
						5	15	25	35	45
						6	16	26	36	46
						7	17	27	37	47
						8	18	28	38	48
						9	19	29	39	49
						10	20	30	40	50

CALLS	TIME	CONTACTS	CALLS	TIME	CONTACTS	THURSDAY 10				
						1	11	21	31	41
						2	12	22	32	42
						3	13	23	33	43
						4	14	24	34	44
						5	15	25	35	45
						6	16	26	36	46
						7	17	27	37	47
						8	18	28	38	48
						9	19	29	39	49
						10	20	30	40	50

CALLS	TIME	CONTACTS	CALLS	TIME	CONTACTS	FRIDAY 11				
						1	11	21	31	41
						2	12	22	32	42
						3	13	23	33	43
						4	14	24	34	44
						5	15	25	35	45
						6	16	26	36	46
						7	17	27	37	47
						8	18	28	38	48
						9	19	29	39	49
						10	20	30	40	50

NOTE: A full size call sheet can be found on page 132 of the appendix. This sheet may be copied for personal use.

If my marketing person whines too much or if he doesn't fax me daily call sheets, one of two things will happen. One option is to forfeit the guarantee and go one hundred percent on commission. If he does that, then I won't ask how many calls he makes or how the day is spent unless he wants me to. He is getting paid on the results he produces. No results, no pay. If not that option, then I will fire him.

When clients are in a slump, they can script their days in five to fifteen minute intervals, pre-plan and then record how they actually spend their time. The insight to be gained from this is invaluable. Productivity is now on purpose.

My coach (yes, I do use a coach) constantly keeps me focused on setting a standard and then holding out for it.

Each week I do the same thing that I ask my clients to do. On Sunday evening, I sit down with my calendar book and predict the week. Let's look at my sample calendar:

Monday, I plan on getting up at 6:00 a.m. and having breakfast. Mondays and Tuesdays are my coaching call days. My first call comes in at 7:25 a.m.; the calls will continue throughout the day. I have a good break from 11:00 a.m. to 1:45 p.m. During this two-hour and forty-five-minute period, I like to go to the gym, read the newspaper and sit in a corner at my favorite restaurant to escape for awhile. At 1:45 p.m., the coaching calls continue. At 6:00 p.m., I'm off to the gym again for the rest of my workout.

Obviously I don't commit to any prospecting calls on Mondays and Tuesdays. Rather, I honor my top priority of my health with two scheduled workouts. I will chart my calories this week, and I carry that chart with me at all times.

I have built in flexibility, Essential Element of Coaching #12, as well. Even though I am planning to go to the gym and then lunch from 11:00 a.m. to 1:45 p.m., I haven't made a commitment to do so. What if an unscheduled interruption comes? What if I need to get out an emergency proposal and demo video to a client who is having a meeting next week and the scheduled speaker just went to the hospital for major surgery.

What am I going to say? I can't get this out right now as I am committed to the gym at this time and then I'm back on coaching calls! That is ridiculous. I will handle the priority and then get back on track. I am committed to workouts. If I miss Monday, I still have plenty of opportunities to fulfill my commitment.

I actually plan to do five, six or seven days of workouts, but I committed to only four in case of unscheduled interruptions (Essential element of coaching #9, coach for reality using MLO's).

You can see Tuesday's anticipated or predicted plan. That doesn't necessarily mean I am going to do those activities. The plan is simply my anticipated outcome and is similar to my airplane example. I have a guidance system that lets me know where I am versus where I had planned to be. For example, let's suppose I don't feel like getting up early on Tuesday morning and stay in bed. But I have a commitment for 90 calls this week and four workouts so I will keep an eye on the rest of the week to make sure I honor my commitment. I have time on Friday to make more calls if I need to since I was planning on quitting at 2:00 p.m. I can also make calls from the airport before my departure and return from my trip to Memphis. If I am on target with my schedule, I probably won't make any calls from the airports. I'll simply relax and take it easy.

What I'm describing is like the automatic thermostat in your home. When it gets too hot, the air conditioner kicks on. When it is too cold, it shuts down. Because I plan in advance for the next seven days, I have a criterion to measure my efforts. I know when I have to push and when I can glide. The reality is that no person can push in high gear 100% of the time. We must build in pace for the long term. High performance goes in cycles.

Everyone in telemarketing knows this. How long can you maintain great focus on the phone before you need a break? Four hours is really stretching it. I would say that a telemarketer needs to have a good push of effort for about three hours, and then at least a thirty-minute break. Follow this with another two or three hour push and you have a productive day.

Back to the calendar. I go over my calendar with my coach. You should do the same with your clients. Have them fax you their weekly calendar and commitment sheets prior to their coaching call.

I am traveling on Wednesday and I have a three-hour program to give on Thursday. This will be followed by travel back to Los Angeles and the drive to Orange County. Then it's back to my normal schedule on Friday. You can see that I have my daughter this weekend, and I have planned to fly to Big Bear for lunch on Saturday and to the beach on Sunday.

This is a very full week. I would rate my intensity level about a seven for this week. An eight would be more calls from the airport, perhaps not taking a breakfast break or even going to the gym during productive time. These are areas where I could be more productive if I needed to or wanted to be. However, I have made a decision to be at a seven for this week. I am on purpose and anchored in reality.

After a brief look at my client's calendar, I next look at their commitment sheet. I want to know if they did everything that they said they would do from last week. If not, what got in the way? Did they lose their priorities? Were they avoiding responsibility? What caused them to not honor their commitments? Perhaps they overcommitted and didn't know it. Perhaps it was 100% the alien; who knows? Clients may not have honored commitments, so I will ask them about their activities. I don't beat people up over not doing what they say they will accomplish. I ask them if they are still willing to honor that commitment because I ask clients to approach their commitments carefully.

I want to have a call that the client is looking forward to, not regretting. At the same time, essential element of coaching #10, coach for accountability, will still be an issue. I want learning to occur. I want to find out what is going on in clients' lives, their perceptions (essential element of coaching #16, coach for process) that had them fall short.

Do you see that this is not beating up the client? My responsibility as a coach is to foster discovery and awareness through questions (essential element of coaching #5). The client knows that when we talk at our scheduled time, I will expect him or her to have done what was on the commitment sheet; but, if the client hasn't, my approach will be to use questions to help generate powerful insights to move forward.

What I have been describing is called "evidence procedure." This means: let's not guess about performance; let's measure it. Measuring performance tends to increase performance. We have to be sensitive about the results trap. This goes to the intuition of the coach. The coach must always be conscious of the temperature of the client. What does the client need right now? What would be best for the client to generate action? Would it be confrontation, telling the truth, or simply congratulating the client for being stuck and letting that client be stuck for the next seven days?

Your clients have different personalities and will respond to you in different ways. For some clients, I put a fine on activities. I ask them for permission to charge their credit card fifty dollars if they don't hire an assistant by the next coaching call, or run four miles three times, or send flowers to their spouse, etc.

For other clients, I will send them flowers. I did this with one client who had a very difficult decision to make regarding a manager in one of her real estate offices. The manager was her friend who did personal sales in addition to managing the office. Through our coaching, it became crystal clear to me and eventually to the client that something had to give. The client wanted a full-time manager and her friend was part-time manager and part-time sales. After our coaching discussion, the owner fired the manager.

That is a good example of **setting a standard and holding out for it.** Sometimes this is not easy to do. This action came from the client, not from me. The solution on her agenda was to fire this person. I helped her to go through the emotions of the alien to stay focused on the action.

I was so proud of my client for taking this stand that I sent her flowers (essential element of coaching #18, champion the client).

These coaching points and examples are enough to get you started coaching. Let's say that you are in a direct marketing organization. One of the guiding principles of many network marketing organizations is to counsel with your upline. I would recommend putting each person in your downline, sales team, office support staff, etc. in a coaching program. Here is how you start.

Fax clients the intake package. Ask them to go through the values clarification, future self and mission statements material. Set a time for them to call you. Make sure that they understand that this is a scheduled appointment and that they have given their word to keep it. Also, make sure that they call you. You don't want to run up a phone bill by calling clients.

On the first call, go over their mission statements and values. Also, on this first call, go over how to fill out their weekly time calendar and commitment sheet. Ask them to fax both of these to you prior to your next call. Finally, set a time to meet seven days from this call.

You will want to talk to them about the philosophies contained in this book. Don't give a client this book until they are experienced enough in their business and with being coached that you think they are ready to coach someone else in their downline. Then, by all means, give them a copy of this book. The client is now a trained rat. Continue to coach them. Coaching can last a lifetime or until the client reaches perfection. As long as you have an interest in their performance and plan on helping them focus, this keeps them in coaching and benefits you.

The principle operating here is called SAID, *Specific Adaptations To Imposed Demands.* The individual will respond to the specific expectations that you impose on them. The moment you stop expecting clients to fax their anticipated outcomes, calendar and commitment sheets, and the moment they know that there is not another person in their corner who does care about what they do this week, performance will fall rapidly.

This principle is from my undergraduate training in health. The body responds to specific demands. Runners look like runners. Have you ever seen a fat tennis player or a skinny offensive lineman? That is why I hold a tremendous amount of hope and energy for my friend Ed. He will lose fifty pounds through a lifestyle change. His body will reduce the cholesterol that is clogging his arteries. He will live for many years.

After you have talked about last week with your clients, then you basically follow them in terms of what issues are important to them. I like to always end my coaching call by examining clients' specific commitments for the next seven days, challenging for MLO's, making sure that they are in alignment with their goals and visions, and then giving them some type of inquiry to think about over the next seven days.

Here is another example of holding the focus. I had another client who had hired a team of assistants to help her do the most productive thing possible, talk to sellers. We developed a list of daily habits, which I recommend you do with all of your clients. Simply ask them what the daily habits are they would like to have that would support them in reaching their goals. I use the word daily the same as weekly because some items might only be done two to three times per week. You still want to focus on them.

This client's daily habits were the following:

1. Carry her call sheets.
2. Coordinate her calendar with her staff.
3. Be in bed by 11:30 p.m. five nights per week.
4. Quality check calls with five to ten buyers per week.
5. Call ten sellers per week.
6. Twenty prospecting calls, new business per week.
7. Exercise: walk thirty minutes per day.

This client had hired one particular person to work with her buyers. This freed her to do more productive activities of prospecting for new business or working with sellers. On one particular call I noticed that she had blocked out three hours to show property for two particular buyers. Do you see an opportunity to do coaching here?

Of course, I confronted her about this. I pointed out earlier in our coaching calls that she described the performances expected from her staff. These included working with buyers. I pointed out that working with buyers was not a part of her daily or weekly habits, and I couldn't see how this was the most productive activity for her. I also pointed out that working with buyers was easier because they had already made the decision to work with her. I suggested that perhaps she was avoiding or rationalizing the task of prospecting.

I hope that you will be this bold with your clients. They really do need to look at what they are doing and how it relates to their purpose, mission, goals, etc.

The result was that she decided not to work with one set of buyers but to continue with the other buyers who were her personal friends. This brings out another coaching element that we haven't talked about yet: **Don't be attached to the result** because it becomes my agenda that she not work with any buyers. All I can do is point things out to her. Look for incongruities and talk about them. Keep her on purpose. Even though I felt she should not have worked with that set of buyers, it was a comfort zone activity. I accepted her decision to do so and moved on.

Depending on how the coaching call has gone, I like to end the conversation with a homework assignment or an inquiry or both. I want the client to be thinking about life for the upcoming week. After all, the client's life is a masterpiece in action and masterpieces take time.

The homework can be things such as going through the marketing plan and writing down ten actions that the client needs to take next week, or writing down three ways to show a spouse your appreciation, etc. Keep a file on each client you are coaching, and ask that person to keep a notebook as well.

Most coaches keep their calls to thirty minutes. This is plenty of time to get into real issues and offer meaningful insights. My first call, the intake call, usually lasts one hour. Coaches have tremendous variety here. Some coaches have a full day of intake, but I don't think that is necessary. Remember, coaching occurs over time. All I want to accomplish on my first call is to create the routine, the system for the coaching to occur and to begin to look at values, visions, goals, and the reality of what is now and what is possible for the future.

I coach each client four weeks per month using thirty minute calls. For months that have five weeks, I don't coach on the fifth week. This gives the professional coach several weeks of vacation.

Inquiries

Why do you always answer a question with another question? Why not?

How can asking powerful questions help your clients focus on issues that are important to them?

Before you answer the question, notice what your mind just did with that question.

Most likely it started to think about the answer. The natural response to a question is a mental and emotional desire to seek the answer.

Webster's Dictionary defines *inquiry* as "a sympathetic investigation of a matter of public interest." *Inquiry*, as practiced by THE COACHES Training Institute is the process of presenting thought-provoking questions for the purpose of introspection and reflection. An *inquiry* is an open question.

To derive the full benefit of an *inquiry*, the client must grapple with the question over time and from a number of different perspectives. *Inquiries have no right or wrong answers.* A powerful *inquiry* will require the client to offer more than one answer. All observations that the client makes regarding the *inquiry* are valid. Thus, an *inquiry* is intended to evoke a deeper understanding, a new perspective, an expansion of possibilities for the client. The coach might pose a question or *inquiry* which points the client in the direction of a new insight or the coach might use an *inquiry* to help the client resolve an impasse.

An *inquiry* offers the client the opportunity to investigate an area of interest that can deepen clients' learnings about themselves and can forward their action toward their goals and vision. One underlying premise of the coaching profession is to forward "human learning, effectiveness and fulfillment." *Inquiry* is one of the major tools used by coaches to encourage learning. During any given coaching session, there are numerous opportunities to deepen the client's learning. *Inquiry* functions best when both the coach and the client have a genuine curiosity about the *inquiry* being offered.

Asking *inquiry* questions requires a coach to see where the client needs to go while maintaining an awareness of where they are in the moment. *Inquiries* can be particularly helpful when they lead the client to the next step. For example, you have a client that has been stuck and unable to move forward. Listening for not only what the client is actually telling you but also for underlying issues can help you formulate a powerful *inquiry* such as, "When you get to this point in the process, what do you allow to sidetrack you from getting what you want?" While there may be one obvious answer to this question, there is a good possibility that the client will generate several more answers that are both surprising and helpful.

Many coaches use an *inquiry* during every session as a means to deepen the client's learning. Often *inquiries* are given at the end of a session to give the client something to think about between sessions. *Inquiries* can be general such as:

What are you tolerating?
What beliefs would you have to give up in order to have your vision come true?
What is challenge?

Or *inquiries* can be created on the spot and applied specifically to an issue that the client is currently working on such as:

Who would you have to be in order to succeed at this goal?
How does fear convince you not to take the next step?
Where in your life do you allow yourself to be a leader?

Inquiry can involve one or more stages. The initial stage of an *inquiry* is for the client to think about the question at various times of the day during the time between sessions. When clients come up with one answer, remind them to look again and see what else they think about the *inquiry*. Sometimes clients may find it helpful to write the question on several post-it notes and place them in various rooms of their houses or offices where they can be reminded of the *inquiry*.

The secondary stage of an *inquiry* can be for clients to write down their thoughts and responses to the *inquiry*. Further insight and understanding can emerge just in the process of committing the thoughts to paper.

The final stage of the *inquiry* can be for clients to fax or mail you their responses prior to the next meeting. This will provide instant *accountability* in regard to the *inquiry* and also allow you to more adequately address the *inquiry* in the following session.

Regardless of whether or not the client writes a response to the *inquiry, inquiries* need to be deferred or discussed at some point in the following session. If you think the *inquiry* is important enough for the client to think about between sessions, then it is important enough to discuss in the following session. Discussion and feedback about the *inquiry* further deepen the learning for the client and also allow space for the coach to acknowledge the client's learning.

Two other subsets of the context of *inquiry* are powerful questions and requests. A powerful question evokes clarity, action, discovery, insight or commitment. "What do you want?" "Who would you have to be to achieve that goal?" "What does that cost you?" are examples of powerful questions. A question that merely seeks information does not qualify as a powerful question. Neither should you confuse powerful questions with some subtle or not-so-subtle attempts to influence your client toward your resolution to a problem. Powerful questions are potent tools employed in furthering clients' agendas, forwarding their actions and deepening their learnings.

Requests

One of the most powerful coaching skills is that of making a *request* of the client. The *request,* extrapolated from the client's agenda, is designed to have the client take actions. A complete *request* includes the person making the *request,* the person receiving the *request,* a specified action, condition of satisfaction (where appropriate) and a completion time and date. The person receiving the *requests* may accept the *request,* decline the *request,* suggest a counteroffer or agree to a future time when the response will be given. Some examples of *requests* are: "Will you schedule a vacation on your calendar by Wednesday?" A *request* differs from a powerful question in that it requires a specific answer (such as "yes" or "no") with an agreement and time to act.

Requesting is a skill that is useful to both coach and client. Frequently, clients will complain about something rather than making a *request* of another person. For example, a client is feeling overwhelmed by having to handle three large projects at work at the same time. She complains to you for feeling tired and overworked, without any hope of feeling better. What *request* could you make of her in order to increase her sense of power in the situation? One possible *request* that you might make of her could be:

"Will you talk to your boss tomorrow about redistributing your work-load?" What *request* could she make of her coworkers that would decrease the amount of work that she faces? Another *request* might be *"Mary, will you create the mailing list of the Smith account by Monday?"*

How can inquiry benefit your clients?

What is the value of looking for more than one answer to an inquiry?

Design an inquiry that would be personally helpful to you right now.

Go through the sample *inquiries* presented here. Make a copy of these inquiries and homework assignments, and put them in your client's file. Put a date next to the one that you ask or the assignment that you give. Make a note that you did so. If you asked the client to put in the time to think about the *inquiry* or to do the homework, the least you can do is remember that you asked them to do so and debrief it on the next call.

SAMPLE INQUIRIES

The following *inquiries* and homework assignments are usually intended for the end of the call. You are asking the client to stick with these assignment or *inquiries* for the week instead of looking for an answer: the client is in a mode of discovery and learning.

SET UP/BEGINNING INQUIRIES:
What do I want? (Practice wanting)
What does it mean to have a full, rich life?
What am I tolerating?
Where am I not being realistic?
What is integrity?
How do I operate?
What is it to live in alignment with my values?
What is it to be powerful?
What is it to be present?
What is my prevalent mood? Is it a habit?
What is choice? What is it to choose?
When do I give myself permission not to keep my word?

What is the difference between a wish and a goal?
Am I being nice or am I being real?
What do I do to avoid feelings? (Booze, food, work, etc.)
Where is my attention? (On self, others, work, daydreams, my vision, values, complaints, etc.)

WHAT WORKS/POSITIVE:
What keeps me going?
What is working?
What frees me up?
What does it mean to be prosperous?
When am I too hard on myself?
What is present when I am at my best?
What is my structure to win or catch myself winning?
In what situation am I the solution?
What is grace, enthusiasm, prosperity, abundance?
What is it to be proactive?
What is it to be centered, optimistic, supportable, non-attached?
What is it to be in the flow, fluid, flexible?
What is to be compassionate?
What is completion? Am I incomplete?
If I only have my attention focused on producing results, what will I have to give up?
Why am I taking this action?

ASSIGNMENTS:
Make _____ mistakes a day, or fail in the attempt.
Take _____ risks this week.
Ask _____ people for the business/out for coffee/a date, etc. each day this week.
Say "so what" _____ times a day.
Answer the question "why bother?" with every new action.
Count the times you speak powerfully.
Only speak powerfully this week (not positively—powerfully). Catch yourself growing (making mistakes).
Identify "jet lag" (when you speak from your past about your thoughts and actions, yet you have grown and changed).
Acquire evidence of some new ability (accomplishments, commitments, being proactive, going for an achievement, etc.).

Choose what you have in every moment.
Have two big belly laughs each day.

ENDING/COMPLETION:
What is it to be complete?
What's next?
What territory have you taken?
How far have you come?
What are the golden nuggets you are taking away?
Who have you become?
What have you built?
What is the new elevation from which you view your life?
What did it take to get there?
What have you learned about yourself?
What does it take to maintain?
What are indicators of yellow-alert signals?
What is momentum?
What will keep you on track?
What is it to be filled with loving kindness?
What is it to live life fully?
What is it to love deeply?
What values require your constant attention?
What will you be giving away?
What is your contribution to the world going to be?
Who did you have to be to reach this place?
How will you know to ask for support?
What acknowledgment would you like to give yourself?

PROACTIVE:
What do I regret or resent?
What am I unwilling to change?
Where might I be in denial?
What am I overlooking?
Where am I taking my foot off the gas?
What is the decision I have been avoiding?
Where do I stop short?
What is a big enough game?
What have I wanted to do but haven't?
What keeps me from winning or succeeding?

Where have I denied myself or others?

Why bother?

What am I being right about?

What complaint, fear, bad habit, discomfort can I do something about today or this week, this month?

Where am I unconscious or asleep?

What am I settling for?

Why this goal? Why bother?

What am I overlooking?

How do I sabotage myself?

What is it to transcend my sense of failures, sense of resignation or feelings of "I can't?"

Where am I selling out on myself?

What am I uncomfortable about doing that I am unwilling to change/willing to change?

What am I stepping over?

What is my reputation?

What do I expect of myself?

ASSIGNMENTS:

Love being alive.

Forgive yourself once a day.

Count the number of times a day you notice the alien.

Be thrilled: over little things, three times a day, with the thing and/or person you dislike.

Laugh/smile 25 times a day and identify 25 things that make you smile/laugh.

Be present for 15 minutes at a time three times a day.

Identify your 5 most prevalent conversations with your alien.

What is the more insidious side of your alien?

Identify your justifications.

Identify your expectations.

Play a bigger game this week.

Eliminate_____words from your vocabulary this week.

Add _____ words to your vocabulary this week.

Do the hard thing first each morning and after lunch.

Say "no" _____ times a day.

STOPPED/BLOCKED CLIENT:
What request(s) can be made to unstick me?
What is the powerful interpretation?
Where am I uncompromising? Where am I too flexible?
What does _____ cost me?
Where do I hold back?
What am I withholding?
Where and what am I unwilling to risk?
What is it to surrender?
Where am I suffering?
What will free me up?
What are my assumptions?
What are my expectations?
What is the Lie?
What am I resisting?
If I were at my best, what would I be doing now?
Where do I give my power away? To whom? When? What are my false
    assumptions?
What/where do I pretend? (to know/to not know?)
What do I need to "let be?"
What's out?
What is needed or wanted in this situation?
What is it to be exceptional?
What will I gather evidence for this week?
What is it to generate or cause?
What are my wants versus my "have to's?"
When am I an automatic NO or YES?
Where do I limit myself?
What are other possibilities?
Where am I too comfortable?
What does it mean to move toward the fear?
What does it meant to "lean into it?"
Where am I selling out on myself?
What ELSE can I do to honor my value?

PLEASURE/FUN/LIGHT:
How can I pamper myself today?
What is it be grateful?
Who can I make smile or laugh this morning/afternoon/eve?

What will recharge my batteries?

What is fun?

How can I contribute to my reserves of fun, leisure, centeredness, balance, resourcefulness, patience, etc.?

How can I have this be easy?

Who can I get to play with me on the project?

What is it to be tickled?

What is grace/serenity?

What makes me laugh/him or her laugh?

Do I choose heavy or do I choose light?

Since I am going to do this any way, do I choose to have it be enjoyable, neutral, hard, or fun?

What can I do to my physical environment to have it nurture me, lighten me up, empower me, etc.?

What is fulfilling, what feels good, and so what?

What is pleasure?

What acknowledgment can I give myself this morn/eve?

What is kindness? What is it to go softly into life?

What is abundance?

How can I make this be playful/light?

How can I double my vitality?

What do I need to give myself permission to do today?

When will I take a break today?

What thrills me?

What does it mean to be awed?

What does it mean to be generous with myself?

What does it mean to be considerate?

What does it mean to be gentle with myself?

What does it mean to gawk/savor?

What am I grateful for this morning/afternoon/eve?

MOTIVATIONAL:

When am I unable to laugh at myself?

What do I have to give up to reach my goals or be a "10?"

What do I choose in any given moment?

What is the distinction between feeling good and fulfillment?

Great goals are compelling: vaguely conceived goals are vaguely manifested—what type are my goals?

What am I building (cathedral or block of stone)?

Who am I becoming?

What is ownership?

What is it to be undauntable?

Who I am is who I say I am — Who am I this week?

What is it to allow or include?

What is it to be creative?

What are powerful questions I can ask myself each morning?

What is it to be tenacious or persistent?

What is it to be passionate?

What flag am I bearing?

What is it to be a leader, powerful, resilient, resourceful, empowering, determined?

What pain do I notice in people around me?

What is it to come from my heart?

How have I withheld myself from life?

Is what I am doing now life affirming or life numbing?

What does it mean to be intuitive?

What does it mean to be focused?

CHAPTER FIVE

How To G.R.O.W. a Client

John Whitmore, in *Coaching For Performance*, gives the acronym G.R.O.W. as a format for asking coaching questions.

G = Goal. What is the *goal* of this call? What do you want to achieve, short term and long term? When do you want to have achieved it? How is it measurable?

R = Reality. What specifically is happening now? Who is involved? What have you done about this so far? What results did that produce? What is happening both internally and externally? What are the major constraints to finding a way forward?

O = Options. What *options* do you have? What else could you do? What if...?

W = Will. What *will* you do? When *will* you do it? *Will* this meet your goal? What *will* you do over the next seven days? What support do you need? Rate yourself on a zero to ten scale on your likelihood of taking this action. What would need to happen for you to rate yourself higher?

This acronym is a template coaches should keep in mind during coaching sessions. As you speak to your clients, you want to be looking at their goals. As you look at your client's goals, you want to compare them to the client's mission, values, previous coaching sessions, etc. You will always be looking for reality and helping the client make doable commitments. The question "What are your *options?*" will constantly flow from you. Of course, you'll also want to anchor your coaching session with, "What will you do this week?"

In my live full-day High Performance Training seminars, I present a four-phase strategy that is a great guide for the coaching process.

Four-Phase Strategy

Phase One: What is Your Goal?

What are the goals that you have in your health, business and personal lives? What specific actions do you need to take by when? What will you do over the next seven days?

Phase Two: What Would Stop You?

I practice more of a tough love philosophy rather than a Pollyanna type of positive attitude approach. I believe in being grounded in reality. Everyone has circumstances that they need to take into account before they make their commitments. Imagine, for example, that you had an elderly parent living at home with you and your help left at 6:00 p.m. each evening. Isn't that a circumstance that should be taken into account before you make a commitment to do volunteer telephone fund-raising for a local charity?

In the calendar I included in this book, I went to Phase Two before I made my prospecting call commitments. I looked at my time restraints and only committed to 90 prospecting calls this week instead of the usual 200.

In this phase, let the alien talk to you. I want to look at my fears, dislikes, circumstances, stories, excuses, etc. This is the place to put all of that on the table before proceeding to Phase Three.

Phase Three: Negotiate

Negotiating is a key phase for it empowers individuals and keeps them in coaching long term. This phase honors circumstances. In Phase Three I will make a deal with the alien. I will negotiate. For example, though I don't like to diet, this week I commit to net less than 1500 calories five out of seven days. I also commit to record the food I eat and to do exercise.

This commitment is a negotiated deal that is referred to as a behavioral contract. This is what I write down on my commitment sheet and fax to my coach. I give very careful thought to my commitments because I have agreed to be held accountable. It is not okay for me to neglect what I say I will do.

Each week for me is different. My time commitments are different, my body feels different, my state of mind is different. I will take all of that into account before I make my deal. Once I have made my deal, I will not let my reasons, feelings, circumstances or other alien stuff stop me. I let all that conversation occur before I make my commitments. Once I have negotiated a deal, I stop any conversations that do not forward the actions.

In my live training, I do an exercise that underscores the power of negotiation. I ask a person with a strong and clearly defined goal to come to the front of the room. For this demonstration, I usually look for a sales person who needs to do prospecting; however, this demo can easily be applied to any situation.

I take this person through Phase One (What is Your Goal?) and Two (What Would Stop You?). I have them identify three obstacles that would compete with the goal. I generally see the following obstacles:

1. I'm too busy with my current business and my priorities to do prospecting.
2. I'm too busy with family commitments to do prospecting.
3. I'm too tired and burned out to continue.

Next, I select three of the biggest men in the audience to come up on stage and represent these obstacles. I put two in front and one person in back.

Now I ask the volunteer to exit the stage. Of course, he can't because his obstacles are holding him back. Next, I take out a hundred dollar bill and tell the volunteer that if he can break free after I say "go," I will give him the bill. What strategy would you use? The most common response is to dig in and try to outmuscle the competitors. This strategy never works long term. It rarely works short term either. If the person selects this strategy, he is doomed to the perception of "I just can't do it." He will live his life in resignation believing the lie that he can't do it.

Most of the time I have "smart rats" who go on their own to Phase

Three. They negotiate a deal with those three people who represent their competing obstacles. "I'll give you each $25 if you let me go." The subject only keeps twenty five dollars, but he has effortless action. He has momentum and inertia.

Phase Four: Reinforcement and Support

In Phase Four, I commit to my coach, request any support that I need and listen to my Baroque Music reinforcement tape. The focus of this book is on the external support of the coaching system, not the internal support from a Largo music tape. However, both parts of the brain need to be reinforced. The left brain is reinforced by the specific commitments we make to our coach. Our coach also reinforces our right brain through emotional inquiries.

The Baroque Music tape is the main reinforcement for my right brain or the emotional side of my brain. I have statements on tape over the music that underscore the type of attitudes and habits that will support my goals. Refer to my book, "The Sky Is Not The Limit—You Are!," for more details on the tape. I suggest that you listen to a tape every day.

I also advocate forming the habit of reading books regularly. So now you have two daily/weekly habits to commit to emotionally: listening to a tape every day and reading a book. Would you commit to those two actions every day this week? How about five out of seven days?

I also highly recommend that you hire a professional coach. If you contact me, I will be glad to refer you to a coach in your desired price range. Expect to pay from two to five hundred dollars per month, depending on the experience level of the coach and the demand for that coach. Life is too short for us not to live fully. Once you are in the coaching program, you will never go back. You will immediately recognize the difference coaching makes in your weekly focus and accomplishments.

CHAPTER SIX

Taming the Alien

"The Alien"

The purpose of this section is to provide a "user's manual" for the brain. I am going to be discussing some psychological paradigms, ways of interpreting what happens to us in life. I first came across many of these techniques while in graduate school in 1977. These ideas are time tested, and easy to follow. They provide a healthy set of guidelines for taming the alien.

Taming The Alien Coaching Point #1
Rational Emotive Therapy (RET)

Albert Ellis is considered the father of rational emotive therapy (RET). RET is a style of thinking that you and your clients will find helpful. I know that somewhere in your coaching you will find the opportunity to offer this RET formula and it will make a world of difference in your clients' abilities to cope with the stress and demands of their lives. What is rational emotive therapy? RET is a structure for internal dialogue. It is training for that internal voice we refer to as the alien. Let's look at some situations to illustrate RET.

Situation #1: I was taking a trip to San Diego one morning to do a series of programs. I would be driving from Irvine to San Diego every day for two weeks. I thought about staying in San Diego, but my programs were over by noon, and I would rather make the drive and pretend that this was a local trip. As I was driving, I looked into my rear view mirror and saw a police car's flashing lights. Immediately, my heart started racing. I glanced down at my speedometer to see how fast I was going. The police car passed me and sped away on another call. I felt a sense of relief. Situation—Police lights on behind me. Feeling—my heart racing.

Situation #2: I am waiting in line at a bank. The teller is new and working slowly. I notice I start to get very anxious. Situation—a line at the bank. Feeling—anxious.

Situation #3: My insurance agent tells me he will make copies of the last two year's tax returns I just gave to him and mail them to me today. Also, he is supposed to get back to me with at least two proposals for disability insurance today, but I haven't heard from him in over a week. I am upset. Situation—delayed response from insurance agent. Feeling—upset, angry.

Situation #4: I agree to take my daughter back to her mother at 7:00 p.m. on Sunday evening after I have had her for the weekend. With that in mind, I schedule one business call at 7:30 p.m. and one coaching call at 8:05 p.m. I go home after a wonderful day with my daughter at about 6:45 p.m. I plan to pick up her bags, clothes etc., but I find a message on my answering service from my ex-wife telling me that she has made plans for the evening and that I need to keep my daughter overnight. I try to call her, but she is not home. Therefore, I cancel my two telephone appointments. Situation—I need to keep my daughter longer than expected. Feeling—anger.

Situation #5: I give an investor $10,000 to help him buy and resell a residential property. He promises to pay me back $11,000 within sixty days. The deal closes, but I never hear from him. I find out that I am not the only person he has stolen from. The police are looking for him. Situation—lost $10,000. Feeling—anger.

I could go on about other situations where I was a victim, or someone took advantage of me. Most people would react to these situations with unwanted anxiety, anger, depression or guilt. RET points out that people are not responding to the situation. They are responding to their beliefs about what has happened to them.

Consider this formula:

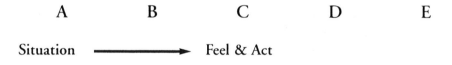

A   B   C   D   E

Situation ———————→ Feel & Act

For most people, the situation (A) leads to how they feel and act (C). As humans we have these four unwanted emotions: anger, depression, anxiety, and guilt. Can you see how the following situations (A's) would lead to unwanted emotions?

1. Traffic.
2. Someone lies to you.
3. Someone fails to keep an appointment.
4. Someone treats you unfairly.
5. A police car pulls you over.
6. Other people don't do what they said they will do.
7. Your children are acting up.
8. Your parents let you down.
9. Spouse.
10. You make a stupid mistake.

11. You are rejected.
12. Someone treats you rudely.

It is easy to fall into the trap of thinking that events, situations or other people make you angry, depressed, anxious or guilty. Rational emotive thinking challenges this type of victim thinking.

$$A \longrightarrow B \longrightarrow C \qquad D \qquad E$$

Situation   Irrational   Feel & Act
               Belief

Here is the rational emotive therapy challenge to the alien. The situation (A) does not lead to feelings and actions (C). The situation (A) is interpreted by irrational beliefs (B). (B) leads to the feelings and actions (C).

The five situations I mentioned are **neutral**. They have no meaning in and of themselves. They are simply facts void of any emotion. In these situations, our alien, our internal dialogue driven by our irrational beliefs, leads us to the unwanted catastrophic feelings. Our irrational beliefs make our perceptions of these situations terrible, horrible, and awful. Below is a list of our ten most common irrational beliefs:

IRRATIONAL BELIEFS
FEEDING THE ALIEN

1. <u>Fear of Rejection</u>
   I must be liked (loved) and respected (approved) by significant others all the time (and it is awful if I am not).

2. <u>Fear of Failure</u>
   I must be thoroughly competent, adequate and achieving at everything I do. Extreme: Perfectionism.

3. <u>Fairness</u>
   People and things should always turn out the way I want them to and I should always be treated fairly (and it is awful when either does not happen).

4. **Blame/Punishment**

   If I am rejected, if I fail, or if I am treated wrongly or badly, then some-one deserves to be strongly blamed or punished. (Sometimes I should blame or punish myself because I decide, "It was my fault.")

5. **Rumination**

   If something seems threatening or fearsome, I must become terribly occupied with it, upset about it, and make myself miserable (anticipatory anxiety).

6. **Perfect Solutions**

   When I don't find quick and easy solutions to my problems, it is awful and horrible. (I can't stand it: A perfect solution exists for every problem.)

7. **Avoidance**

   I find life easier when I avoid difficulties, responsibilities, and uncomfortable situations than when I face them.

8. **I am not Responsible**

   People and external things make me feel the way I do (upset me, make me miserable) and I have little ability to direct and control my feelings.

9. **Past Conditioning**

   Your past remains all important and, because something once strongly influenced your life, it continues to determine your feelings and behavior today.

10. **Detachment**

    You can achieve happiness (safety or security) by getting involved in and doing nothing or by passively and uncommitedly "living."

What irrational beliefs are being focused on in these five RET situations?

Situation #1: The fact is that the lights go on behind me. My irrational thinking is, "It's not fair and I must always be treated fairly. What about all of those cars going faster than I am? I don't want to get a ticket. My insurance rates will increase, etc."

Situation #2: The fact is that I am waiting in line. The irrational belief is "I must never be delayed; if I am, that's terrible."

Situation #3: The fact is that my insurance agent is not reacting as fast as I would like. He has promised things that he has not produced. The irrational beliefs are, "People should move at the pace I want; if they don't, that's terrible. All people should do what they say they'll do."

Situation #4: The fact is that my ex-wife was not at home at 7:00 p.m. on Sunday evening. Nothing else about this situation is part of the facts. My being upset is due to my irrational belief that focuses on her not honoring our agreement. "She put her own needs in front of our daughter's. We have an agreement and everyone must always honor their word."

Situation #5: The fact is that I lost $10,000. The irrational beliefs operating here are that I must never be lied to and that all people must be honest.

A way to perceive all of these situations that will produce less anxiety, anger, depression and guilt is to expand on the ABCDE model.

Here is the intervention based on the above formula: a situation occurs and that is the fact. Instead of accepting the irrational beliefs, go to (D) and dispute the irrational beliefs. The procedure is to think, "Although I would prefer for people to be honest, do what they say they will do, etc.," they will not always behave this way. With this procedure,

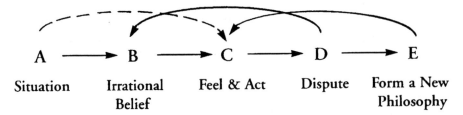

you have just disputed your irrational belief. Next, go to (E) and change the way you feel and act by forming a new philosophy.

Use this format: "Although I would prefer that all people are honest, I recognize that some people are not. It is not catastrophic if they are not." To explain this I'll describe four steps in "cognitive restructuring."

FOUR STEPS IN COGNITIVE RESTRUCTURING

❑ **Step 1**

Identify the internal dialogue (thoughts) in a specific situation that lead to excessive or unwanted anxiety, anger, depression or guilt.

Identify thoughts about:
   a) yourself.
   b) the others involved.
   c) the situation.

❑ **Step 2**

Identify any of the ten irrational ideas that might be supporting the alien thinking in Step 1.

❑ **Step 3**

Challenge any irrational or rationalized thinking in Steps 1 and 2 by identifying or asking:

   a) What is true that you are thinking?
   b) What is not true that you are thinking?
   c) What about any potential catastrophe? ("What if...." "It would be awful..."), or absolute thinking ("I <u>must</u>, I <u>should</u>...").

❑ **Step 4**

Substitute specific rational thoughts that lead to less anxiety, anger, depression or guilt. These thoughts must be <u>true</u> and be directly counter to the thoughts that were disruptive.

The Formula

This is not necessarily an easy formula to use. However, what options do you have? Life is too short to be caught up in the terror of irrational beliefs. We can choose to use RET and greatly reduce the stress from the facts and events. Let's look at our physiological reactions to stress in the following chart:

PHYSIOLOGICAL REACTIONS TO STRESS

Stomach secretes excessive acid that eventually leads to ulcers.

Chemical changes accelerate the aging process.

Shifts in hormone balance cause skin disorders, certain allergic reactions, asthma, and hardening of the arteries.

Heart rate doubles, contributing to heart failure.

Adrenaline increases, causing numbness, trembling, dizziness, fatigue, paralysis, and breathing difficulties.

Pupils dilate involuntarily, perspiration increases, saliva and mucus secretions decrease.

Blood pressure rises, possibly leading to stroke or hypertension.

Muscle tightening causes arthritis as well as certain stomach and intestinal disorders.

Facial muscle contortions force nasal and throat passages open, leading to hyperventilation.

Blood clots more easily, leading to phlebitis, heart attacks, and strokes.

Blood sugar level rises, putting strain on the pancreas.

Pent Up Anger causes depression, decreases lymphocytes, decreased antibodies, increased susceptibility to disease, and a physiological chain of effects.

YOUR PERFORMANCE IS A PHYSIOLOGICAL STATE. SET THE CONDITIONS FOR HIGH ACHIEVEMENT WITH THE RIGHT PHYSIOLOGICAL STATE!

We have a choice of how to react to stress. We must take responsibility, make choices that will promote peace of mind, and forward the action. I am sure that you will find instances when you can fax this concept to your clients to help them make better sense of the world and handle stressful situations more positively.

Taming the Alien Coaching Point #2
Eliminate the *I Have To's*.

This is more training for the alien. A technique I use in my live programs is to ask the audience to place their right hands directly over their faces. This represents the alien, the fear-based internal dialogue gripping and leading them. Then, I ask the group to use their left hands and grab the alien and pull it off their faces. I ask them to talk to the alien and tell it the following: "Thank you for caring but not for sharing."

The alien is designed to avoid and justify the avoidance with rationalization. In this chapter, we are redesigning the alien conversation with a user's manual. So, coaching point #2 is another subtle distinction to be made to lessen the grip of the alien. Instead, ask yourself, "What do I have to do?" What do you tell yourself that you have to do?

> ❏ I have to go to work.
> ❏ I have to eat.
> ❏ I have to exercise.
> ❏ I have to prospect.
> ❏ I have to get this project finished.
> ❏ I have to pay taxes.
> ❏ I have to be in a relationship.

The response to all of these is a big, "NO, YOU DON'T!" You don't have to do anything. You can choose. Certain results will follow if you don't take certain actions. If you don't go to work, you might get fired and lose your income but you don't have to go to work. You don't have to eat. If you don't, you will get sick and die but you don't have to eat. It might seem silly to carry this to the extreme. However, this is a subtle distinction that will reduce pressure and stress.

There is an optimal level of pressure, stress and effort that will produce an optimal level of performance. Above or below that level, performance will decrease. Each of us knows how that optimal level feels. We have all experienced being in the flow. This means being "on" where nothing could stop us and where we could effortlessly perform. Athletes refer to this as being in the "zone."

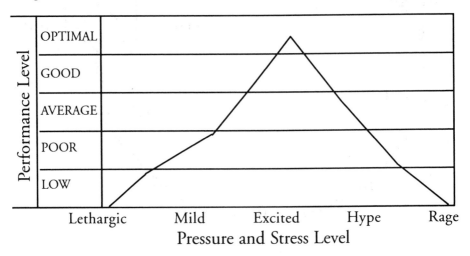

The subtle distinctions that are in this chapter will help all of us to stay in that "zone." The focus, clarity, and accountability from being in a coaching program will help keep us in that zone. Let's look at a metaphor that will help you feel the results of the "I have to" paradigm.

Imagine you are enclosed in a box that is slightly larger than you are. Describe how you would feel. What words come to mind? Closed in, claustrophobic, fearful, hot, anxious, like you want to break out. This is what you do to yourself when you have the internal dialogue of "I have to." Look at this scenario as it applies to the "I have to" of DIET-ING...I have to <u>DIET!</u>

You are going to make yourself diet to lose weight. You have to diet. You have to count calories, stay away from fat and begin an exercise program. You can't have dessert, you can't have pie. So you put yourself into the psychological box where you feel trapped, lonely, and frustrated.

The world is against you. All you think about is food. You turn on the TV and see a commercial for pie. You immediately turn it off. You pick

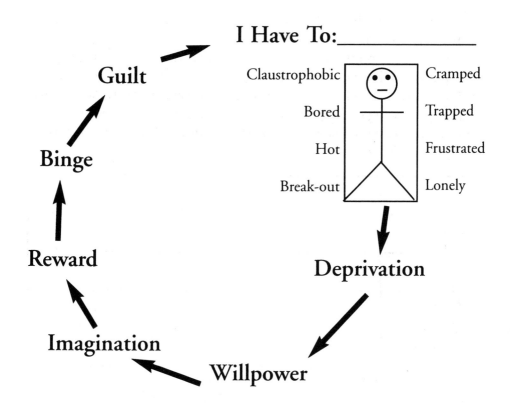

up the newspaper and open to a full page ad for pie. You put it down. You go into the refrigerator for some bottled water and find a huge piece of pie with your name on it looking at you. Your mind is dominated by what you can't have.

You have heard of this principle before. Try not to think of the color green. You can't help thinking of it. You are now in the state labeled "deprivation." You are, however, determined to stay on your diet. So you now are using all of the willpower you have to maintain this deprived state. Next, your imagination and the alien begin a conversation like this:

"You've been dieting for so long now. You are starved. You are a good person. You deserve to eat today, just today. Your weight is doing fine. It won't hurt you just to treat yourself this one time. I love you. Food loves you."

Willpower is associated with deprivation. Imagination is associated with reward. When the two are in conflict, which one do you think will win out? That's right—reward.

So you leave town and head for the first all-you-can-eat buffet you can find. You start loading up on everything. You eat everything that is not fake. You even eat your sheet that you were using to count your calories. You hear people saying, "Hurry up! Here he comes again." Mothers are grabbing their young to protect them from the undertow you create at the buffet line. Someone says, "Grab a piece of chicken and run for it. Everyone save themselves!"

You sit at a booth by yourself determined to put new meaning into the word "all" in all-you-can-eat buffet. The manager comes over to you and asks if you are waiting for someone else and if you are eating for them too! You get thrown out of an all-you-can-eat buffet for eating too much! You just had a **binge!**

What follows a binge? You guessed it—**guilt.** "What did I do? I was doing so well on my diet. I am so disgusted with myself. That's it. I have to diet." Now you are right back where you started: back into the psychological prison.

There is a way to break this negative, self-defeating cycle. Eliminate a link in the cycle. Eliminate the have to's. Make choices. You don't have to do anything. You can eat whatever you want in whatever amounts you want to.

Take responsibility for the consequences of your choices. If you overeat, you will be fat. That's it! If you want to lose weight, make the choice to eat less and exercise more for the next seven days. Be very specific about what eating less and exercising more means.

Thinking like this really does make a difference. You will remove pressure when you do. I'll give you some personal examples. Writing this book is one. I had been gathering information from THE COACHES Training Institute and other sources of coaching ideas for the last two years with this book in mind. That was not a delay or procrastination: it was necessary research (alien talk!). I had the information I needed for this book, but the alien freaked out.

Here was the alien's conversation:

"You are too busy booking yourself for next year's speaking engagements. Even though you have a full time marketing director and you are booked by several speakers bureaus, untapped opportunities still exist for you to book yourself. You can't get too many bookings. You have to prospect. The book will have to wait.

True Lies

This is a "**true lie.**" I do benefit from my own prospecting. I have trained myself to enjoy prospecting. I am good at it and I do produce results at a fee of $6,500.00 for speaking engagements. The truth is that the effort I spend prospecting will be my income eight months to a year later.

That part is true. Here is the lie. If I stop prospecting long enough to devote full time to writing this book, my business will suffer tremendously, momentum will be lost, and I will lose money. What a lie it is!

I ask my coaching clients what lies they are living and find their answers are revealing. The process involves an inquiry: What do I need to say "yes" to and what do I need to say "no" to? Another inquiry is: What does it mean to surrender?

I made a choice to surrender my business prospecting, to say "no" to being an employee in my business. Instead, I chose to work on my business, for this book will be another feather in my cap for credibility. This book will help people like you who are in a position to be of great value to other human beings to earn a living. It will bring me passive income, and it does not require me to get on an airplane.

This book will be a contribution to the field of professional coaching. Writing this book is one of the most productive activities that I could be doing. I had to surrender to prospecting, however, to free myself up to write. I had to say "no" to being in the office making outbound prospecting calls.

The same is true for another project in my life. I am a private pilot rated to fly by what is called visual flight rules (VFR). This means that I need to be free of clouds to fly. If John Wayne Airport has a marine layer covering the airport, my destination might be clear, but I cannot receive a clearance to depart John Wayne until visual flight rules apply. In this case, it is inconvenient; however, in other cases, it could be dangerous. Let's say that I am already in Las Vegas. I call for a weather briefing, and the forecast for my time of arrival is for clear skies. The forecast turns out to be wrong. By the time I approach the airport, a solid overcast has moved in, and I can't land. I only have thirty minutes of fuel left and need to find an alternate airport to land.

Nothing is unsafe about flying through clouds as long as you are trained to do so. I kept thinking, "**I have to** get my IFR training." This is another one of those "I have to's."

By thinking like this, I was putting tremendous pressure on myself. It affected my prospecting because I resented being unable to do the things I wanted to do as I was tied down to prospecting. You can imagine that I started to build up resentment towards my marketing director. "Other speakers' marketing reps can keep them fully booked; why can't you completely fill my calendar?"

True lies! *True,* I will be a much better and safer pilot when I have my IFR rating. *Lies,* I am too busy to do it. Essential element of coaching #6 says, "Tell the truth." My coach helped me to see what I didn't want to see. I was more comfortable being stuck in the struggle of wanting to write a book, becoming IFR rated, etc. than taking the actions to get things done. I had some fears and it was going to be difficult. Perhaps I couldn't do it: the fears were feeding the alien.

When you confront fears, they usually step aside: they are illusions. Consider skydiving as an example. When I bring clients out to experience a tandem skydive, they are sometimes so filled with fear that I have to physically take them to the airport. Once they actually do the jump, they are filled with exhilaration, joy, self-confidence and pride. This accomplishment represents a low point for the alien!

Confronting my fears, I have decided to take the month of August off to write my book. I will do the same for my IFR rating by taking off the month of December. True, I will be behind in my marketing; however, in a short period of time I will catch up with the lost time in marketing and have a book and an instrument rating.

The "I have to's" do not produce action. Instead, they produce frustration. Frustration leads to short-term actions driven by willpower and this willpower falls victim to imagination. This is followed by abuse of time, food, etc. Finally, guilt sets in and then the cycle is repeated. Surrender!

I have another interesting personal story about surrendering and letting go of "I have to's." I was consistently 10 to 20 pounds heavier than I wanted to be. I have always exercised and selected the right type of foods, but I have always eaten too much. I was addicted to diet Cokes and low-fat, sugar-free yogurt. After a firm conversation with the alien, I gathered up all of my suits and went to the tailor to have them "re-fitted" for the new, heavier me. Within three weeks after I did that, I lost twenty pounds because I didn't have to! This stuff works as a user's manual for the brain! With great pride I went back to the tailors with my suits after losing 40 pounds! Where in your life could you benefit from letting go of the "I have to's" and surrendering?

Here and Now

The "Here and Now" is one of my favorite concepts for producing action and change. This concept can be illustrated with a story that goes back to my college coaching days at Cal State Fullerton. In 1979, the Titan Athletic Foundation (TAF) was the athletic fundraising arm for the university. Our motto was "We do so much more with so much less." Our goal was to raise $300,000. I remember our first "team" meeting where we had a goal to have raised at least $125,000. Our actual numbers after all of the team players' pledges were counted was $75,000.

In violation of the "here and now" concept, everyone immediately began to compare our work to last year's fund drive. The previous year our goal had been $200,000. We had $85,000 in cash pledges that year. This was looking to the **past**. Then, we projected to the **future**. Our goal was $100,000 higher than last year. At the same time the previous year, we were $10,000 higher in pledges then we were this year. How were we ever going to reach our goal?

Fear, panic and disbelief immediately set in and momentum ceased. How much fundraising do you think that the group went through over the next couple of weeks? Not much.

The learning is that the only thing you and I can control is our present. We can't control the past; we can't control the future; we can only work in the now. When we project to the future, we often panic. When we go back to the past, we panic. We must stay in the here and now!

Put this concept in your toolkit to compete with the alien. The alien wants you to float all over the place to keep you from the area that will produce action, the present. The reason that the alien wants you to do this is because it is in partnership with your "survival mechanism" designed to protect you. If you do take action, you will compete with your comfort zone and produce change. Change is one of the three major forms of resistance. We resist doing activities we don't feel like doing, we resist doing activities that we perceive to be uncomfortable, and we resist and fear change.

The safest place to be is in the past or future. Stay in the here and now!

Another example of "here and now" comes from my experiences with exercise. When I made the decision that I was going to start running again, I was not in great shape. I decided to run Turtle Rock Drive, in Irvine, California. This is a four-mile loop in the area where I live. The loop offers variety because it has flat parts, slight inclines and declines, and steep hills as well. In the direction that I decided to run, the last mile is a steady incline.

Off I went! I made three miles before fatigue really hit me at the beginning of a steady incline. I can vividly remember my thinking: the alien said, "I have another mile to go. I am very tired. Maybe I should just start walking. My knees feel okay but I am physically exhausted. Look at how far I have to go. I can't do it. I've run too far, too soon. I'm going to die!"

Pure alien vision! Poor me! This is what happens when you go back and forth from the past to the future. I applied the principle: "I am going to focus on going to that landmark about fifty yards up the hill. Now, my mind is on counting each step to reach that landmark. After I reach that landmark, I will set another one and then count steps [immediate present] again." After doing this for about three landmarks, I was home! If I kept my focus in the future, I promise you I would not have made it. Using this concept also works for marketing.

A promoter for my one-day seminars lost her telemarketer. She had to get on the phone herself and book her own presentations. (The first barrier in her thinking was, "I have to.") Her first day of calls was relatively pleasant, and she booked four appointments. Then, the reality of rejection set in. She became very upset and projected to the future. "I can't stand this. I am getting no response on the phone. People are rude and one person even hung up on me. How am I ever going to set enough appointments to sell 100 people into our next public seminar? I've already made fifty calls today and haven't booked anything. How am I going to pay my bills? I'm going to die!"

PANIC, PANIC, PANIC, PANIC, PANIC, PANIC, PANIC, PANIC!

The key is to stay focused on this one call, then the next call, etc. As a coach, when you catch your clients in a panic, this is one of the techniques you can point out to help them remain focused and active.

Contingencies

Contingencies are another coaching intervention that produce immediate focus and immediate results. Contingencies come in this format:

After I _____ then,_____.
        stated measurable action   *stated measurable reward*

Use the same format to substitute **If**, followed by the action, and **then**, followed by the reward. For example:

If <u>I make five more prospecting calls</u>, **then** <u>I will go out to lunch</u>.
     stated measurable action   *stated measurable reward*

For my daughter, Danielle, the contingency is: **If** you clean up your room and pick up all your toys and put them away neatly, **then** we can go to the pool.

The if/then, after/then contingencies format works great because it breaks down actions into small increments that are measurable. Also, success is immediately followed by a reward. The reward can be small such as making a personal call, reading your E-mail, grabbing a piece of fruit, or the reward can be large such as taking a vacation, buying a new computer, etc.

You can use this with your clients by grabbing a big item and breaking it down into small manageable pieces, putting the pieces into a contingency format. Then, challenge or request your clients to take a series of actions and select some type of reward to be enjoyed after they have completed those actions.

Rewards and Punishments

Rewards and punishments are examples of classical conditioning. We live in a stimulus–response world that can be described by an experiment. The goal of the experiment is to have a pigeon in a box run to the back wall and press a lever for food.

When the pigeon is placed in the box, it pecks haphazardly. The researcher draws a line on the floor. When the pigeon randomly crosses over that line, the researcher drops a food pellet into the box. The hungry pigeon eats the pellet and is removed from the box.

Another line is drawn on the floor closer to the back wall, and the pigeon is again placed in the box. When the pigeon randomly goes past the second line, another food pellet is dropped into the box. The procedure is repeated and the line is moved closer and closer to the desired back wall. Eventually, the pigeon will enter this box and run immediately to the back wall. When it reaches the box, it will not be fed until it randomly pecks at the lever on the wall. After a few trials, the pigeon is now conditioned to enter the box, go immediately to the back wall, and press the lever for food.

This is an example of rewards and punishments in action. The reward is to be given for a prescribed behavior. On the other hand, the punishment is not receiving food until the desired behavior is performed. The experiment also illustrates the extinguishing of one set of rules, crossing the line, and establishing another, pecking at the lever. Crossing the line will no longer produce the same result as in the past, for a new standard applies.

A practical application for this concept and your coaching is to help the client place their future vision, their mission statement, and their stated goals and activities into weekly commitments. Then, set in motion tangible rewards for taking those actions. Get agreements for the actions and for the rewards or, in some cases, punishments.

Many times it is appropriate for me to use fines as a punishment. I'll challenge the client, "If you don't do this activity, would you send me $50?" The client's response gives me information. If the client waivers on this, where is their attention? The client's attention is on not accomplishing the goal. Either the client is not really committed to the goal or perhaps the commitment is too big. That means I need to make the discovery and awareness clear for them. Usually, the way that I do this is to ask the client what they think is underneath the hesitation to make that $50 commitment. Then, I'll ask how much of that commitment the client would be willing to put $50 on (reality-based coaching).

Be careful with using fines. If you feel that your client would respond to fines, they can definitely put an exclamation point on commitments. How would you know if your clients would respond favorably to the use of fines? ASK THEM!

CHAPTER SEVEN

How to Set Up the Weekly Coaching Call

First, who are you going to coach? A friend who is committed to business, health and personal fulfillment? A coworker or employee? Someone in your organization who would benefit from an improvement in their performance?

Why are you going to coach? What is the benefit to you? I request that you are very clear on this. Once you have answered this question, then simply call your client and set a phone appointment. My first coaching call with a client is what I refer to as an "intake" call. I allow one hour for that call. The procedures I use are included in the intake portion of this book. Keep in mind that you shouldn't try to get it all done in one call. Remember, coaching for optimal results occurs over time. If you feel incomplete on your coaching call, you can always give the client homework to do and go over it on your next call.

Each call after intake lasts 30 minutes. I usually start with a review of what we talked about the previous week. I let the client make any comments as I go over my notes. Sometimes I go back over my notes from two weeks back. Next, I will ask clients for a temperature checkup. I ask them to rate their state of mind and body on a zero to ten scale. If I don't get any low numbers, I ask clients about any pressing issues that may have occurred since our last call or if something is on their mind that they would like to discuss.

After discussions that are client initiated, we will look at their daily/weekly habits and commitments from the previous week to look at accomplishments. At this time, I am looking for more than accountability. I am looking for the processes that either supported or prevented clients from reaching their goals. Then, we review their commitments for the next seven days. As a committed coach, I want to uncover any hidden agendas, blocks, or challenges to their perceived commitments.

If nothing specific comes up, we might be at the end of our 30-minute call. If that is the case, I will either give the client a homework assignment or an inquiry to stimulate some insightful thinking over the next seven days. Then, I make sure that I set the time for the next call before ending the one I'm on.

Some coaching calls will reveal great insights, discoveries, learning and breakthroughs. On some calls, a client may go into tears as they uncover fears and blocks. Some calls will reveal where your clients are selling out, or what they are tolerating, or what they need to say "no" to, etc. The effect of such calls will be profound for a coaching client.

Likewise, some coaching calls may leave you wondering if you are giving the client any real value. Some calls may be nothing more than accountability check-in calls. That is alright. You don't have to be brilliant on every call. Don't set yourself up for disappointment because you **are** helping your client. You have them in a system of outcomes with a method of reinforcement and support. You have them constantly looking at how they can improve. You are helping your client in ways that remain to be seen. The miracles and great intuitive insights will show themselves in your coaching. Be patient and consistent and, above all, always hold the greater vision for your client. Also, remember that the responsibility for moving forward with the coaching call remains with the client—not you. Ask your client, "What coaching would you give yourself right now to create value on this call?"

CHAPTER EIGHT

Coaching in Athletics and Coaching in life

As you probably already know, my background includes coaching football and wrestling. Much of the philosophy that I have revealed to you in this book came from coaching experiences. Working with Jeff Blatnick for two years was a learning experience. Coaching athletes at Cal State Fullerton was a learning experience. I owe much of the development of my principles to the coaches who I worked with at Fullerton. Gene Murphy, Bob Burt, Roger Thomas, Steve Mariucci, Jerry Brown, Richard Smith, Richard Ellerson, Greg Newhouse, and Larry Manful have all had a hand in the development of these philosophies.

The coaching profession is characterized by a strong work ethic. I can remember our staff meetings at 7:00 a.m. on Mondays during the season, followed by a meeting of the defensive coaches from 8:00 until 10:30 a.m. This was followed by preparation work by individual coaches through lunch and then group meetings at 2:30 p.m. with practice from 3:15 until 5:45 p.m. Dinner was followed by more staff meetings to evaluate the day's practice, continue studying the opponent, application of our game plan, and preparation for the rest of the week. I would usually leave for home at about 1:30 a.m. and repeat the same cycle on Tuesdays and Wednesdays.

From coaching I learned to be passionate about work. I also learned an appreciation for time control. **Everything** we did was scripted. We scripted our two-and-one-half hour practices into five-minute intervals. I even scripted my five-minute intervals into one-minute segments. Each activity was preplanned. When we gathered with the scout team offense to run the opponent's plays against our defense, that was scripted. Each play was put on cards for the scout team to run (scout team was a group of our players simulating the opponent). Each coach had a script of the play and the defense formation. Everything was planned in advance.

Unfortunately, all these plans did not give us the competitive advantage because every coaching staff and team we competed against was doing the same thing. Athletic coaching is a good way to show precise planning. I remember the summer camps before the beginning of our season. We met and did the equivalent of business planning. We created our system for defense and then put our installation schedule in the calendar. As a staff, we had our entire summer camp planned in advance. We also reevaluated daily and made adjustments simultaneously.

In athletic coaching, as in industry, we had a chain of command.

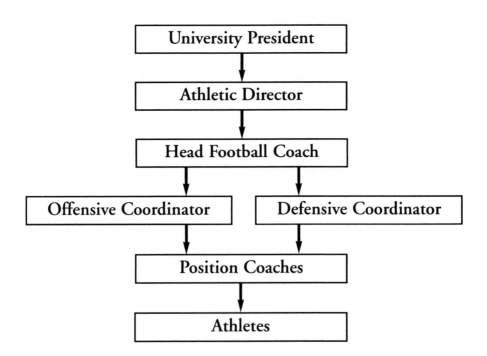

Each level had its own roles, responsibilities, and accountabilities. If a company had the same type of planning that a football team uses, it would be an efficient, top-producing company. The hierarchy was filled with passionate individuals who were committed to a common goal. Everything associated with coaching was fast paced, highly motivated, and passionate. Powerful camaraderie existed among the players and coaches. Being part of a team meant something very special.

When I left coaching in 1983, I thought I would find these attributes in the business world. I thought that everyone would be highly committed, well prepared, highly motivated, and competitive. I mistakenly thought that when I walked into a company's office I would be able to feel the teamwork.

Imagine my surprise at what I found. I'll give you an example. I was the featured speaker at an annual kickoff function for the regional meeting of a real-estate franchise. After speaking to the group for over two hours, I wanted to illustrate how circumstances would affect the reality of our commitments. I asked a gentleman sitting up front to tell me a specific activity he was planning to do over the next seven days. He couldn't do it. He didn't have any idea what specific actions he would take over the next seven days. I was stunned.

Here was an independent contractor, business owner, commission-only salesperson without a marketing plan or installation schedule. I probed further, and he finally came up with a commitment to knock on 500 doors in his territory that week.

I tested for reality:

Coach: *"How many doors did you knock on last week?"*

Client: "**None.**"

Coach: *"How about the week before?"*

Client: "**None.**"

Coach: *"Would you be satisfied if you knocked on only half of the 500 doors this week?"*

Client: "**Sure.**"

Coach: *"How about if you only knocked on 100 doors? Would that be a good number?"*

Client: **"Yes."**

Coach: *"Would you pay me $100 if you don't knock on 100 doors this week?"*

Client: **"No, it might snow."**

Coach: *"What amount of door knocking would you commit to no matter what?"*

Client: **"Well, I guess about 25."**

I have a hunch that the amount of doors this person will knock on this week is zero. What do you think?

This guy was in desperate trouble. How do you think his production is? How many people do you think would offer him money for his marketing plan?

I didn't spend too much time with him. Fortunately, I was an experienced speaker at the time of this example, and I didn't want to embarrass him in front of the group or waste the group's time with a poor example.

When I returned to California, I called the director of training for that company. I told him how concerned I was about that interaction and asked how representative that person was of the entire group. We agreed on a word that would describe the preparation of the average salesperson:

Pathetic!

There are many parallels between good coaching and good business. Athletic teams have team goals and individual goals. These goals are agreed upon before the season begins. Each team member has his or her individual role to fill. These roles define a team: 11 individuals who have interrelated roles. As each individual fills a role, the team as a whole has an accomplishment. In athletics, we were part of a system and, if we executed our responsibility, the system worked to perfection.

The diagram represents a half line with the X's and 0's on offense and the letters representing the end, tackle, nose guard and linebacker on

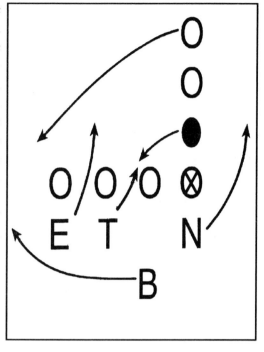

defense (B). With action to the defense's left, the correct action for the linebacker is to scrape off the defensive end's position. This is how the system works because, in this defense, the players in front of him are slanting to the inside. If the linebacker doesn't perform his role, his responsibility, then the system breaks down.

The same is true for any company. Each individual has a role to fill. What if **B** isn't motivated and doesn't feel like performing his role in the system? Everything breaks down at the expense of those who are performing their responsibilities.

In a real-estate company, the owner has a fixed overhead. The owner pays for the building, phone lines, secretary, electricity, franchise fees, etc. The company has goals and the support necessary to gain the market share it is committed to. The company projects a budget based on the anticipated sales efforts of the realtors on the same team. Training, advertising, and other items are all budgeted based on an assumption that the salespeople will execute their roles. If they don't, then the system fails.

I always wondered why businesses are not like football teams with their planning and commitment levels. Finally, I gained an insight. It seems to be related to ease of entry. Not everyone can be a football player. To be a division one, scholarship football player, every athlete was required to demonstrate previous success. Each athlete on our team was the best player on his high school team. Each athlete had years of sacrifice to achieve his goals. The noncommitted athletes were simply weeded out.

The business equivalent to this would be for salespeople to qualify at some production level before they could be accepted in an office. Once accepted, because of supply and demand, they would be replaced each year by new people if they didn't meet a certain level of production. Under this set of circumstances, you would certainly find a different level of commitment. If people weren't motivated or committed, they would fire themselves.

Many companies today have minimum production levels. This is a principle of coaching, setting a standard and holding out for that standard. If this is done, word will get out. Instead of scaring people off, the company will attract good people. Why? Because people crave accountability.

Why didn't the manager of the real-estate office with the person mentioned earlier know that this person was not prepared? Who is tolerating a manager who is not on top of their salespeople? What is the "food chain" here? Sales agent, manager, trainer, regional director, owner.

The sales agent is not at fault. I blame the person most directly supervising his performance. Even though that person is an independent contractor, responsible for his or her own performance, he or she is part of a team and someone is responsible for performing that role. The manager is at fault. Next, I blame the trainer, who has the responsibility to make sure that each link of the system is aligned. Is that trainer delivering the training necessary for the manager to control his biggest asset, the salespeople? Then, I blame the regional director, and so on.

The problem is that blaming doesn't matter. I remember a lesson I learned a long time ago as a coach. Our staff was watching films of our team, Cal State Fullerton, against the University of Arizona. On one particular pass play, one of my players, an outside linebacker, was supposed to drop to an area called the flat, a wide area zone. Instead, he dropped deep and narrow into an area called the curl zone. The pass was completed in the area that he should have been in, which led to a touchdown that eventually led to our losing the game. I reacted by yelling, "I can't believe him. We practiced this every day."

The defensive coordinator interrupted me and said something I will never forget: "Don't blame the kid; blame yourself. I hold you responsible for the way he plays. He did what you coached him to do. Look to the way you are coaching if you worked on this and he still drops to the wrong area!"

What a dose of accountability! This has led to the development of a fundamental core of my coaching, that is, I ask each client to commit to the daily habit of accountability and to practice being accountable. I ask all clients to buy into the concept that they are the source of all that they experience. They need to look to themselves as the cause of everything that happens to them.

In athletics, coaching taught me to make time special. Coaching also taught me to break the tasks into their basic elements. Not only would we practice tackling but also we would break down all of the skills necessary to complete the task. We would practice our stance, first steps, rolling the hips, head across the numbers for an angle tackle, grabbing jerseys, etc. Each element was practiced, drilled, and rehearsed so that in the game it all came naturally and without thought.

Clients you coach will have goals that they want to accomplish in their health, business, and personal lives. In the role of coach, your gift to the client is to help them break these areas down into their component parts and then commit to actions over the next seven days.

I have a variation of a four-step strategy that I use with clients who are overwhelmed. This involves the principle of breaking down the task into manageable parts.

❏ CATEGORIES

❏ ACTIONS

❏ PRIORITIES

❏ COMMITMENTS OVER NEXT SEVEN DAYS

I ask clients to identify the categories in their lives that need their attention individually. Next, I ask them to mindmap the actions that are necessary to solve those problems or create the results. Then, I ask the client to prioritize those actions and commit to those actions that they will take over the next seven days. This reminds me of the planning an athletic coach does for an installation schedule.

All of the coaches on the original Cal State Fullerton staff have gone on to bigger and better challenges. Richard Smith is an assistant coach in the NFL. Jerry Brown was instrumental in bringing Northwestern to the 1995 Rose Bowl game against USC. Steve Mariucci was the guiding force helping Green Bay packers quarterback Brett Farve to become the 1995 Most Valuable Player for the NFL. Steve has since left Green Bay to become the head coach of the San Francisco 49ers.

I recently visited with Steve and asked him several questions regarding the parallels between athletic coaching and business.

Interview with Steve Mariucci, Head Coach
San Francisco 49ers, Berkley, California

Bob Davies: You coached at Cal twice. Your first stint there won a bowl game. You left them with quality players and a winning tradition. Still, in your absence there was a losing program that resulted in several losing seasons. What does it take to have a consistently winning program?

Steve Mariucci: *I found the team frustrated, not reaching its goals and not disciplined. Most of this I attribute to a lack of continuity with coaching staffs. Marv Levy, who has gone to four Super Bowls, was there and only won a handful of games. He had Bill Walsh, John Ralston, and Mike White on his staff. I can't tell you how many awesome coaches have been there and haven't won. I think no other staff has been there long enough to develop the continuity necessary to put in their system and win.*

Davies: Coming in as a new staff member, what are the most important factors or building blocks that must be put into place to turn around this Cal program and make it a winning program?

Marriucci: *Right from the beginning, we established that every athlete would be treated the same—whether the guy is a walk-on or a starter, we expect accountability. It's the off-season, but we still work out at 6:30 a.m., six days a week. The guys know they will all be dealt with in the same way and they will be held accountable.*

Davies: You've coached on several different levels, from college to the pros with the L. A. Rams, Green Bay Packers, and now the San Francisco 49ers. What would you say is the most common trait of the consistently great athletes?

Marriucci: *Reggie White, Sterling Sharpe, Bret Farve ... what separates them is their work ethic. They are very conscious of taking care of their bodies year round. Sterling Sharpe used to lift weights on game day. Reggie White was always on the stairmaster to keep his weight down. We had Reggie and his wife over for dinner. When I asked about dessert, his wife answered and said "NO! He's a fanatic about his body." That focus allows the great ones to work through an injury, to practice when they hurt. They master their bodies.*

Davies: At the elite level, everyone is good. What separates the good from the great?

Mariucci: *Elite performers don't settle for "good" in anything. They expect to play great. They expect to practice hard. They have high expectations and combine it with a high work ethic.*

NOTES

CHAPTER NINE

Success Stories

I owe this personal success story to the focus and accountability that I received from my coach at the time, Mike Grumet. Several years ago, Mike, who is not a professionally trained coach, was my "accountability" partner. Since that time I have hired a professional coach. I am still great friends with Mike, and I continue to help him stay focused.

Sunday evening I committed to Mike that I would take my daughter, Danielle, camping over the upcoming weekend. By Friday I would buy a tent, sleeping bags, etc. and we would drive to the San Diego campsite late Friday afternoon and stay through Sunday afternoon.

I thought that it would be a great weekend, and I was looking forward to going. My alien, however, started doing its thing. I realized Thursday I hadn't gone to the sporting goods store to buy the equipment. That was no problem; I could do that tomorrow. Friday finally arrived. The alien greeted me with these thoughts, "You really don't want to do this. First of all, you are going to spend all this money on equipment and only use it one time. What a waste! Also, you are not very patient with Danielle. You have never spent that much time with her by yourself. You might get angry, yell at her, and hurt your relationship. You would accomplish the same thing just by staying home and going to the pool. She really likes the pool. Don't go! Stay home!"

Very compelling thoughts. After all, I don't want to be selfish. I need to think of Danielle's needs first. This is the conversation I was going through. However, because of coaching, I had some competitive thoughts as well.

"I have already committed to Mike that I will go. He will be there with his children, and they are looking forward to seeing Danielle. I'm the person who is always screaming at Mike to do what he says he will do. I said I would do this and I will."

Do you see how the alien was aligned with avoiding fear? The statement that I have made all along is that fears are lies. So I purchased the camping gear, we loaded up my car, and off we went to San Diego.

It was great! We had a wonderful time. I will always be thankful to coaching for that special time I spent with my little girl. We talked and played all night in the tent. We played "monsters" with the flashlights. We thought it was starting to rain on us until we realized we were actually next to a sprinkler. We toasted marshmallows over the fire.

I will never forget the joy in my daughter's eyes as she helped me put up the tent. If it wasn't for someone holding out for me to honor my word and to break through my fears, I know exactly what I would have done. I would have stayed home and gone to the association pool for a couple of hours. Then I would have brought Danielle home, put on a video, and gone into my home office to work. I would have rationalized that I was spending quality time with my daughter and getting some work done as well. What a lie. Thank you, Mike, and thank you coaching!

Testimonial from Mike Grumet
New York Life, Huntington Beach, California

I have learned the following long-term lessons from my coaching experience with Bob Davies:

How to—
1. be accountable for my activities.
2. measure my performance.
3. set realistic goals on a (weekly) basis.
4. overcome fear.
5. organize my life in a meaningful way.

While I was in advertising, I overcame the fear of approaching new industries not represented in my magazine. During my final quarter of sales, I set records, most of it from an industry other reps would not touch.

I overcame the fear of giving up a client base developed over 13 years and a substantial income for an opportunity to help people in the new career of financial services. I am taking slow and steady steps to build a lifelong clientele. In the meantime, as a result of early success with the business community, my new employee has hired me an assistant to book appointments for my special business niche.

I am confident that with your coaching I will double or triple my income from my previous career within three years.

In addition to my career development, I am a much happier and active person. I sit on two fund raising boards and the YMCA board for Indian Guides. I also help on committees of all types. In addition, I still make time for my family and friends. I will never forget the look on my wife's face when I surprised her with over 100 friends and family at a restaurant for her birthday.

I owe the success of that surprise party and the joy of the accomplishment to the focus I received from your coaching. I was able to handle multiple priorities and still get them all finished.

Through coaching, I have found time and energy to be a PARTICIPANT in life instead of an OBSERVER.

The following success story is not related to professional and personal coaching. Rather, it is about athletic coaching and demonstrates the essential element of coaching #14, stretch your clients.

From Lynn Rogers, Head Womans Gymnastics Coach Cal State Fullerton, Fullerton, California

I recruited a very talented gymnast from Canada, Carol Johnson. Carol was a unique athlete. She was born with only one arm. I didn't have any expectations for her on bars and vaulting, but she would be excellent on the floor exercise and the balance beam.

In practice she always wanted to work the bars and she always wanted to do the vault. The crowd liked her. It was fun to work with her but, at the same time, it was getting down to crunch time. We were getting ready for the national championships and the bigger meets. It was always a bit awkward having Carol in the gym because she wanted attention, and I'd rather be spending my time with my big guns, the kids that could really do the skills and help us get the points.

At this same time, I had a rookie assistant coach, Breck, a former Cal State Fullerton football player. He didn't know much about gymnastics and I had to teach him too. Teaching Breck and trying to work with Carol became very difficult on certain events because I was trying to go full speed someplace else.

One day Carol decided she wanted to learn a trick on the bars. She wanted to learn to flip between the bars. I knew enough about gymnastics to know that a kid with one arm was never going to do that trick. Because Breck didn't know enough about gymnastics, he wanted to try to teach it to her. Well, that was heaven for me. Here I had a coach who was willing to take this kid out of my group and work with her. This would allow me to run with my fast kids.

Carol actually did learn the trick. And she learned it because she didn't have any mental limitations. Breck also didn't have any limitations because he didn't know that she wasn't able to do the trick. I'll always remember that story because it was a valuable lesson for me. My experience was a negative factor in that situation. I didn't set my goals high enough since I didn't think it could be done. Carol did it all because she was such an exceptional human being and gymnast. Breck was also an exceptional human being who was willing to trust her.

This really hit home. I don't think anyone should put limits on anyone else. Stretch your clients!

Bob, you mention a lot about setting a standard and holding out for it. Another story quickly comes to mind that illustrates that point. We had a girl that came out from Colorado to California, never having been away from home. She was very talented, and we had high expectations for this athlete. She got homesick, gained a lot of weight, and got frustrated with her gymnastics. These two factors went hand in hand. She was upset about being away from home so she began overeating. The resulting weight limited her ability to participate in gymnastics. As a result, she went into a downward spiral. She got discouraged in her class work, so she ate more. This, in turn, affected her gymnastics. A vicious cycle was created: she was really going down in a hurry.

I haven't done this very often but, at the end of the year, we took her off scholarship. She was clearly not holding up her end of the bargain. Her parents were not happy, she wasn't happy, and we were seen as the bad guys for doing what we did.

She went home to Colorado, and I didn't see her for quite awhile. About eight months later a young lady walked into the gym. I didn't recognize her. This was a lean, strong, healthy young lady. As she came closer, her face seemed familiar. It was the kid that we had kicked off the team minus about 25 pounds. I didn't know what to expect.

She came up to me and said, "I came back to California for one reason. I wanted to tell you something."

I braced myself. I'm nuts thinking, "This kid is going to tell me she's going to sue me." I had no idea about where she was coming from.

She said, "I want to say 'thank you'. You turned my life around." I said, "Excuse me?" and she said, "I went home and I was so miserable, but I took a look in the mirror and I realized that it was me that made myself so miserable. I let myself down, my family down, my team down. I didn't deserve a scholarship. I deserved to get kicked off that team. I want you to know that last semester I made straight A's in school and I lost 25 pounds.

I've got a boyfriend now, life is really good, and I owe that to you! If I had stayed in California, I would probably still be sinking."

Thank you, Lynn, for sharing that inspirational story. What an example of setting a standard and holding out for it. I have to congratulate Lynn and his staff for doing what was best for his "client," firing her. It would have been easier to sit in his own comfort zone by not taking this action or to give her one more in a series of last chances. Lynn didn't do it. That is one of the reasons why Lynn has had Cal State Fullerton Women's Gymnastics team in more regional and national championships than any other program in the country. Coaching makes the difference.

Lynn will always remember this story because he set a standard and held out for it. Many times he was encouraged to "lower the bar" so that more kids could go over.

This reminds me of a client that I fired. This particular person had the attitude that since her company was paying me to coach her I was responsible for her getting results. She refused to participate in the coaching. She did not complete the homework assignments and inquiries that I gave her. She was not willing to look at her resistance either. I took a stand and fired her as a client. I told her company that I would not work with her and gave them a refund for the unused portion of her monthly coaching fee.

The result was almost identical to Lynn's example. My action served as a wakeup call for her. She finally decided to participate and complete the requests I gave her. She made some important decisions that she had put off making in favor of whining, complaining, and blaming. She said my being strong and firing her was what she needed to get moving. I appreciated that since I wasn't sure I had done the right thing. I then referred her to another coach, and she continued with a new appreciation for her possibilities.

It really helps to create a standard with your clients and then to hold out for that standard. As Lynn says, "If you want to win, you must have accountability because everyone skates, including me."

You also need to be strong as a coach. Never <u>need</u> a client; always <u>want</u> one. Thomas Leonard of Coach University says, "Always shoot for more earnings than you actually need: this way you will not be afraid to lose a client."

The same principle applies for those of you in management. Always coach from what you know is right, not out of fear that your "client" might quit.

I asked Lynn one last question, "Do you have any slogans that you use with your team to rally them?" His response was, "Take no prisoners." I asked him to explain.

"When you are on the last event, the floor exercise, don't start cruising because you think we have already won the meet. Go hard till the very end, until the meet is over.

Jane Cocking, From Human Energy Resources Roswell, Georgia

I was training a group of people to be trainers for a coaching program in a major international corporation. The participants had a variety of experience levels. We were in a group of four people, and we were working on training in different parts of the program.

One woman was very timid. Her voice was not strong and her body language was not confident. Everything about her said that she was not confident. A short while into her presentation, I stopped her. I asked her "What are you aware of right now?" She said that she was aware that her voice wasn't strong, that she could hear her voice shaking. She couldn't think about what she was saying, and she didn't feel confident.

I asked her, "On a scale of zero to ten, where is your confidence level right now?" She put it at a three. I asked her, "Where would you want it to be considering that this is your first time?" She said that she wanted it to be at least an eight and eventually a ten.

The next question I asked her was, "What would it sound like if you were at an eight right now?" She totally changed. Her voice was confident; it wasn't shaking. She was totally focused on what she said. She burst into tears. She recognized the difference and that she could do it. The next day she was leading a part of the program, and she related that story. It was a life-changing moment because confidence was something she had struggled with for a long time. The power was in recognizing that she could do it in one minute. If she could do it once, she then could do it again.

Teri E. Belf, M.A., C.A.G.S.,
From Success Unlimited Network
A coaches training and certification company
Reston, Virginia

Living in the Questions: ON PURPOSE

If you had told my client, Ellen, that in five months she would have a new career, be successfully employed as an entrepreneur, have transformed her relationship with her son, and have found her perfect partner, she would have directed you to the nearest psychiatric hospital. Yet, this is exactly what happened during her coaching program.

Ellen came to me wanting to find the courage to go for her dreams. She felt she had lofty dreams. She would discover that dreams are merely pre-realities of the future she could create and did create.

Presenting Circumstances

Safe corporate environments had been home for this single parent for 18 years when, suddenly, the day before Thanksgiving, she found herself among the unemployed with a mortgage and a 15-year-old teenager. Although Ellen was usually able to boldly march ahead with her life, this event felt overwhelming. At age 41, her courage faltered and her future appeared blurry. Ellen sought a coach to guide her process.

Her coach began by helping her uncover her life purpose, create visions, lifetime and annual goals. At first, Ellen found it difficult to identify what she wanted although she definitely knew what she did not want. Through repetitious questioning, her coach guided her to unveil what she had been afraid to surface. Persistently her coach would ask, "What do you want?" "What do you really want?" Questions bombarded her, session after session (sessions ran 2 hours, every other week for eight meetings total). After enough questions, Ellen adopted the habit of asking herself the same questions. By the end of five months, she knew how to make purposeful choices, and the results she imagined were hers.

Career

To help Ellen get in touch with her career dreams, her coach had her examine her worklife, past and present, to note what she truly loved to do best. Two of her prized activities had been individual staff meetings (in which she felt free to converse about an employee's whole life, not just on-the-job responsibilities) and teaching the Course in Self-Management. As Training Director she had delegated other training programs to staff yet reserved this favorite class for herself. Her explorations delved into the meaning of work, values, qualities, and interests. Ellen was asked to put her awareness on what intrigued her.

Ellen's fear of becoming an entrepreneur centered on her belief that to be on your own meant to sacrifice those delightful benefits that had fringed her 18-year management career. "Ask three external consultants what they do for benefits," suggested her coach. Armed with relevant information, she garnered the courage to join the growing group of for-mer middle managers disappearing into the flowering fields of home-based businesses… in a career that manifested her life purpose.

Family

The inquiry method worked again to help Ellen get in touch with her bottom line regarding the daily control battles she experienced with her son, Allen. The already familiar questions, "What do you want?" resound-ed loudly in Ellen's ears. "Name everything that bothers you, and then pick the three things that head the list," offered her coach. Ellen used to make a big deal about everything. For her next step, she carefully chose her battles based upon what is most important to her.

Her coach also helped her formulate a question to use when faced with an upcoming disagreement. The self-directed question aids Ellen to distinguish herself, "Is this my 'stuff' or his 'stuff'?" before entering into potentially argumentative conversations with her son, husband, or anyone else.

After Ellen learned her life purpose, "to inspire and guide people to take steps toward their dreams," her coach asked her to examine every area of her life, such as fun, friends, service, health, etc. and note the extent to which she was living on purpose. As she explored her life, she was express-ing her purposefulness with her friends and her staff at work, and she rec-ognized that she was not inspiring her son. Her coach asked her to brain-storm ways of living on purpose with Allen and do one of them. At Allen's suggestion, they playfully sauntered outside to the patio outfitted with charcoal crayons. Under Allen's direction, the patio began to transform into a multidimensional solar system. Truly inspiring to the designers were the process as well as the outcome; inspirational adventures became a hallmark of their new relationship. Ellen's newest learning—purposeful experiences can be intentional.

Relationship

For 15 years Ellen had searched for her perfect partner. Her list of what she did not want in a relationship grew and grew. When her coach asked her what she wanted in a relationship, she drew a blank. She spent all her time adding to her list of what she did not want. But what she wanted??? After several hours with much discussion and clarification, Ellen could finally verbalize what she wanted in a relationship and how that relationship would complement and enhance her life purpose. Her coach concluded by asking, "When will you meet this person?" AND the phone rang.

The rest is history. Ellen's caller was someone she had met twice in the previous four years yet missed opportunities right under her nose because she was not focused on what she wanted. Now happily married, Ellen learned a powerful lesson to stay focused on what she wants.

Coaching does not mean changing our lives; it means changing the questions we ask ourselves. It means answering the questions through the visor of our life purpose so we can experience the satisfaction and fulfillment we deserve. Ellen's experience with the coaching process is characteristic of the successes possible for anyone, for everyone.

Penny Stephens, Goal-Tenders
Seal Beach, California

One of my very first clients was a real estate agent. Chris had been working as a full-time agent for three years with marginal success. What she kept saying was, "I guess I'll have to go get a real job!" (That meant a 9-5 job.) She was too scared to set a goal around a dollar amount that she wanted to earn, so we worked with what she was comfortable with. She thought she could sell two houses each month and was willing to set a goal of selling 24 houses in a twelve-month period.

Chris liked to farm, and she just loved talking with people as long as she could dress comfortably and the temperature was under 87 degrees. Of course, I didn't realize those were the ground rules until we got into summer and that became her "excuse," but I'm getting ahead of myself.

The commitments I asked Chris to make were on a weekly basis and the activity that she had control of. She agreed to farm three days per week, four hours each day, and hold one open house per weekend. For weeks I heard of some success along with every excuse imaginable. Chris had a lot of resistance to success to overcome.

At one point in the processing of commitments not kept, Chris realized that she didn't like working with sellers because she felt they were too demanding. She had been giving away an average of $500 per sale from her commission on disputes between the seller and buyer. We worked on the theory that she was just the messenger, carrying information back and forth between the seller and buyer. Presenting options to her clients, helping them make their own decisions was the way Chris was able to let each transaction close without her investment.

She also resisted making listing presentations because she was uncomfortable about not knowing enough. We worked through her beliefs about having all the answers by setting up the wonderful opportunity to go back and talk with prospects with information they are asking for. Even if you have all the answers, you may decide not to tell all so you can schedule that time to get back to them with additional information.

What a success Chris had! She earned $75,000 that year, which was more money than she had made in the previous three years together.

New Client

The challenge: Build a new company to $120,000 gross revenues in the first year. The owner, an entrepreneur, whose strength was technical/mathematical, task oriented, is required to sell product and service.

John's goal for each month was $10,000 in new business. When I asked John what his commitments were around getting new business for the week, he said, "I'm getting 5 referrals from my present client base and I'll talk with 10 prospects about my company."

Qualifications for commitment:

1. Is your commitment specific and measurable, one that you can take action on?
2. Is your commitment a stretch and realistic to you?
3. Can you see yourself keeping your commitments?

If the answer is "no" to any of these questions, I ask my client to reconsider, and be kind to themselves while they stretch to do new things.

In this instance, John hung on to his commitment. He was excited and surprised that I was willing to ask him to make and write down his goals that were specific, measurable, actionable, realistic, and tinted.

At our next meeting, John quickly confessed he had not kept his commitments. He explained, however, that he had gotten three referrals and made contact with four new people. He had gotten two new clients, one a referral, and the other from the prospects he spoke with. He was elated because he could see the value in making the calls.

After holding John accountable to his commitment, he was clear about how uncomfortable he was as the salesperson. I asked if he wanted to recommit to the same commitment. He quickly agreed. I then asked him to agree to pay me $5 for each referral and prospect call he didn't make. Instead, he agreed to give me my choice of software worth $100. Product has more importance to John, so this would give him more of an incentive.

John kept his commitment to call for 5 referrals and he spoke with 27 new prospects. I was curious if his bet with me was what motivated him to make the calls. It wasn't that at all. At our very first meeting I mentioned that it's helpful to keep a "Success Journal," in book form or on 3x5 cards. He went straight home and found an old spiral bound book of 3x5 cards. After tearing out the old used cards he began to write about those clients that he had "Sold." And there were many of them. He didn't go into great detail; writing "SOLD and the name of the company" was enough to remind him.

During that next week, when he got scared and questioned whether he could sell his service and product, he would look through those cards to be reassured of his past successes. Needless to say, he is feeling much more self-confident about his selling abilities. And he met his $10,000 new business goal for the month.

CHAPTER TEN

Conclusion

I remember being in Bakersfield at the Days Inn prior to a seminar. It was late in the evening, and I was lying in bed watching the news just before dozing off to sleep. Suddenly, the fire alarm sounded. At first I ignored it. I had heard false alarms before. But when I heard some sounds outside my door, I casually opened the door. I saw nothing but smoke in the hallway. "Oh my God! This is for real." What happened next was interesting. In the panic, I had the presence of mind to grab my Piaget watch, wallet, and workout shorts. The watch went on first, then the shorts. My wallet was in a fanny pack pouch so that went on next.

As I entered the hallway, I was disoriented. I went to the left. An elevator was there but no exit. The other people in the hallway and I turned around to go in the other direction looking for an exit. The smoke was incredibly thick. I couldn't breath. I was just about to hit the ground for some clean air when I saw the stairwell. I went into the stairwell and outside to safety.

Although one person was overcome by smoke and taken to the hospital, everyone else made it out without incident. The actual damage to the hotel was minimal. It turns out that some curtains had caught fire from a faulty air conditioner in the hallway.

No one knew if this was a serious fire or not at its onset. I can remember thinking as I stood outside that I could have been killed. I was in tears as I thought about my daughter and the problems I was having with my ex-wife. I could only think how petty all my problems really were. This experience put things in perspective for me.

To put things in perspective for clients, ask them if they were to die today what regrets they would have in their lives. When I asked myself that question, my answer was clear. I had not been spending enough time with my daughter.

Please make a note and highlight the above inquiry. Go back to the section in this book on inquiries on page 63 and write that one in. In the future, I would be grateful for you to fax me any inquiries that you develop that I could use with my clients. My fax number is 949-830-9492.

First came insight, then the decision, then the commitment, and then the action. This led me to stop marketing myself in a way that put me on the road 100% of the time. I had to face the illusions of my fears so I could change the way I was doing business. My fears proved to be lies. I made the changes necessary so that today I travel about one third as much as I used to. Today I have a great relationship with my daughter.

Coaching creates this awareness at warp speed. Coaching creates client inertia. A body in motion will remain in motion unless acted upon by an external force. Likewise, any body at rest will remain at rest unless acted upon by an external force. You are the external force!

You give a gift through coaching. You give the gift of hope, enthusiasm, respect, empowerment, joy, confidence, challenge, and love. You invite your clients to play a bigger game and to embrace and erase fear.

Do you remember the legendary Alabama football coach Bear Bryant? Coach Bryant said that he would die when he stopped coaching. Do you know how long he lived after he retired? He died within six months of retiring. What was different about retirement? The biggest difference was that he no longer had a plan, a challenge and seven days to implement the plan.

When you and I are striving to achieve a goal, we have a shift in the electrical activity in our brains. Using a CAT scan, doctors can actually see which area of the brain is electrically active. For instance, show a patient a picture and the visual area is active. Start playing music and there is a shift of electrical activity to the auditory area.

When we are depressed, the electrical stimulation is in the area of the limbic system called the amygdala. This shuts down the receptor cites for endorphins. This also shuts down the release of endorphins. Endorphins are the body's natural morphine. In fact, endorphins, chains of amino acids, have the same molecular structure as morphine. When we have a natural release of endorphins, we are enthusiastic, motivated and feel great. You have heard this referred to as the "runner's high." We are in the "zone." We have heightened performances.

This is what happens when a person is in a coaching program. Making specific commitments to a coach sets the stage. The rest of the week is the challenge of handling life's priorities, crises, and interruptions and still do what you said you would do. Simply the possibility of being 100% for the week and doing what you said you would do creates this physiology.

Fear is the illusion that we all must fight through. Even the most well intentioned and most disciplined individual will fall victim to fear and to lies. Coaching can make the difference. Ask your clients to have zero tolerance for whatever is stopping them from making decisions and moving forward. Don't let your clients play victim roles. Don't let them get away with, "I don't know what to do." A sale is going to be made. They are either going to sell you the reasons why they can't do it or you are going to sell them the vision and opportunity to get things done.

Ask your clients what they need to <u>accept</u> and what they need to <u>reject</u>. People get overwhelmed because they take on too much. Don't let your clients do that. Never get attached to their outcomes. They are responsible for their successes, but stay strong for them. Hold higher expectations for your clients than they do for themselves.

Once you feel comfortable with coaching and using the techniques put forth in this book, feel free to add your own agenda into your coaching sessions. Feel free to ask for permission to give your opinion; never impose your opinion, but feel free to offer it. Put your personality into your coaching. Be a source of accountability, commitment, focus and clarity.

You may wear several hats other than that of coach for your clients. You might be a trainer, teaching them what to do and how to do it. You might be a counselor, attempting to find out what deep-seated patterns are present from earlier experiences and are still blocking them. Recognize when you are not wearing the "coaching" hat.

Do not impose coaching. You offer a gift which they can accept or reject. Be nonjudgmental and maintain confidentiality.

Above all else, please do not wait until you have it down and are good to start coaching another person. This book is designed to help the business person coach another individual. It is not designed to teach you to be a professional paid coach. For that training, call THE COACHES Training Institute. Use this book as a guideline for immediate impact.

There is no such thing as a bad coach. Simply the conversation about an individual's life will produce results. The eighteen essential elements in this book will set you on the path to immediate impact with your clients. Remember, the word "clients" means those individuals that you are committed to as a coach.

Here is an example about the statement, "there is no such thing as a bad coach." I was in a coach's training workshop and was partnered with a woman who had a poor self-image (she said so). She was not experienced and was intimidated to be working with me since I am a trainer. She had absolutely no idea how to coach. However, she was an attentive student in the program, and she remembered the skill she had been taught to use whenever she was stuck, had no idea what direction to go or what to say. This skill was simply to repeat these phrases:

"Tell me more about that."

"What are your options?"

"What will you do?"

"What actions will you take over the next seven days?"

That's exactly what she did. I told her my situation and the only words she mumbled were those four questions over and over again.

I came out with three excellent solutions that I was not aware of prior to this practice role play. I thanked her for being such an excellent coach. There is no such thing as a bad coach. You can be a better coach using these beginning principles, but there is no such thing as a bad coach. So please, don't wait to start until you "get it." Start now. Create a masterpiece! Coach for life! Be guided by love and goodness! Coach with integrity and unselfishness. Walk your talk. Hire a professional coach for yourself.

Thank you for reading this book. Keep it as a ready reference at all times. Read this book again and take notes. You are ready to coach. Now go to it. Use your talent and

COACH FOR HIGH PERFORMANCE!

Appendix:

The Revelation—A Revealing Truth

What does it mean to be passionate? Look at the word passion. Break it into its component parts; pass "I" on. What are you excited about and what are you becoming that you are passing on to others? I can't remember who said this about the word passion. I heard it when I was speaking at the first annual Professional and Personal Coaches Association conference.

What does it mean to be obsessed? Is it bad to be obsessed? The question itself seems to hint at something bad. Consider this. What if you were obsessed with prosperity, helping others, and still being healthy and having balance? What if you were obsessed in your business, health, and personal life? Is this possible? Yes!

The truth is that systems work. Coaching works. Presetting outcomes with internal and external support for clarity and accountability works. Life works. The amazing revelation is that whatever is not working in your life can be fixed with the proper system.

The proper system refers to precise planning, time prediction, and action accountability. No matter what the situation is, this formula will produce the results you decide to have.

An important issue for you and for almost all of your clients will be the personal matter of health and, more specifically, weight control. Since this is such a universal issue, I decided to end this book with my simple system for guaranteed weight control. I will not be as specific as I am in my "Healthy Living" audiocassette album; however, I will be precise, to the point, and action oriented to a level where I can guarantee that if you follow these words of wisdom, you and your clients will achieve lifetime weight control.

If you control your weight anything from losing that last five pounds you have been rationalizing about to losing a necessary 50 pounds, the benefits to you could fill a book. Those benefits will range from increased energy and self-esteem to a sense of euphoria and dramatically increased productivity.

Here is the simple shortcut I personally follow and request of my clients. Eat anything you want to and as much as you want. Go ahead; I'm not kidding. Eat as much as you want. The only thing I ask you to do is

Bob Davies Calorie Counter

MONDAY

Time	Food	Calories	Exercise
		Total	Intake
		Minus	Expend
		Equals	Net

FRIDAY

Time	Food	Calories	Exercise
		Total	Intake
		Minus	Expend
		Equals	Net

TUESDAY

Time	Food	Calories	Exercise
		Total	Intake
		Minus	Expend
		Equals	Net

SATURDAY

Time	Food	Calories	Exercise
		Total	Intake
		Minus	Expend
		Equals	Net

WEDNESDAY

Time	Food	Calories	Exercise
		Total	Intake
		Minus	Expend
		Equals	Net

SUNDAY

Time	Food	Calories	Exercise
		Total	Intake
		Minus	Expend
		Equals	Net

THURSDAY

Time	Food	Calories	Exercise
		Total	Intake
		Minus	Expend
		Equals	Net

Day	Calories	Exercise	Net
Monday			
Tuesday			
Wednesday			
Thursday			
Friday			
Saturday			
Sunday			
Total			

to record what time it is, what food you eat and estimate how many calories you take in for each item you put in your mouth. I also ask you to record the estimate from your exercise and have a net every day. My philosophy is to estimate high on intake, low on expenditures.

If you are not sure whether yogurt has 300 or 350 calories, record the higher amount. If you're not sure that a two-mile walk burns 150 or 250 calories, record 150. That's it. Eat whatever you want and as much as you want as long as you record it.

Please refer to the sample recording chart on page 124. This becomes one of the daily habits that I create with clients. In some cases I ask clients to fax their sheets to me for accountability.

This discipline produces measurable intake accountability. There is no guesswork. One pound of fat is equal to 3,500 calories. Here is a formula that is a reasonable estimate:

Your body weight x 10 = amount of calories needed to maintain that body weight. If you want to lose one pound per week then subtract 500 calories from that amount and net out to that amount daily.

Example: 190 pounds body weight x 10 = 1900 calories received daily to maintain that weight. Also, 1400 calories daily for seven days means losing one pound. That is it. Simple!

Monday, I get up at 5:30 a.m. and go to the gym to lift weights. I don't count any calories for lifting because I am burning muscle glycogen (sugar) and because I am honoring the rule to estimate low for expenditure. Then, I get on the stairmaster exercise machine for 30 minutes and burn 520 calories. I record those calories for Monday in the exercise column. Then, I go to breakfast and eat a light meal of 250 calories and have all of the no calorie beverage that I want. I am not hungry, I feel full and go into the office. I have a reasonable lunch around noon and record 500 calories. That brings me to 750 calories against my exercise of 520 netting out to +230 calories. Looking good. I have all kinds of choices now. I can go to the gym again in the evening and burn another 300-500+ calories, or I can skip the gym and still have nearly 1200 calories to spare for my evening meal plus snacks.

In my particular situation, I would go to the gym again, burn another 300 calories bringing me to 820 calories burned against only 750 calories intake. I have a nice dinner, even overeating slightly and take in 1500 calories with my evening meal for a total of 2250 calories. I deduct 820 calories and net out to 1430, which is almost where I need to be to lose one pound and I overate in the evening.

This is measurable productivity and I am in control. There is no deprivation—only conscious choices. The deal starts again on Tuesday as I start all over again with a clean slate of zero calories and continue to make choices. I am in control.

No matter what happens, always record your intake and expenditure. Your mind will automatically begin to make choices as your eating becomes conscious, not automatic. You will cut down your intake and increase your expenditure automatically without the use of willpower.

One catch is that you need your coach to hold you accountable to count your calories. Every calorie from a healthy apple to a handful of fat-free pretzels must be counted.

This system works: it will produce long-term weight loss.

Nutrition and Weight loss

According to the U.S. government, almost 56% of all Americans are overweight, and one in three of these is considered clinically obese, that is, over 30% above their ideal weight. The primary cause of this is that, as a nation, we exercise far less and eat much more than we did in the past. Obesity is connected to cardiovascular disease, cancer, heart failure, diabetes, hypertension, reduced life expectancy and poorer quality of life.

If you are overweight, it is serious. The solution is a lifestyle of exercise with proper nutrition.

Weight Loss vs. Fat Loss

An important link to exercise when it comes to weight loss is weight training, which builds lean or muscle mass. This increases your metabolic rate, causing calories to be burned faster. Eating less, however, decreases your metabolic rate particularly on a starvation type diet or a chemically induced appetite suppression program.

Extremely low calorie diets also cause a starvation reaction during which the body holds on to stored fat because it contains more calories. You actually burn lean muscle and organ tissue for energy. True fat loss can only occur at a rate of one to two pounds per week.

Rules for Eating Properly

If you are similar to most people, you have less than ideal eating habits. There is no realistic way for you to rearrange your lifestyle and stick with the new lifestyle long enough to make the difference you want. Therefore, make yourself some priorities.

First, start an exercise program and consistently record your expenditure. Next, add the following recommendations into your lifestyle.

1. Increase fiber. Fiber is filling and reduces blood pressure and cholesterol. Even heart disease, which kills over 50% of Americans, is linked to increased fiber in the diet. The recommended daily amount is 25+ grams.

2. Decrease fat and saturated fat. The American Cancer Society has linked many forms of cancer to high fat intake.

3. Decrease dietary cholesterol. High blood cholesterol is considered the number one risk factor associated with heart disease.

4. Decrease refined sugar. Sugar increases your appetite by increasing the secretion of insulin. This results in low blood sugar and leaves you craving the rise again. Refined sugar in foods such as candy adds no nutritional value but lots of empty calories.

5. Decrease salt. Lowering your salt intake is good for your blood pressure. It also helps in reducing the risk of heart disease and certain cancers.

6. Increase water intake. Your body weight is 60% water. It is the medium for every reaction in the body. As a general rule, consume one ounce of water for every two pounds of body weight. For most people this would come to 2 quarts per day.

Follow these simple recommendations and understand that a magical diet does not exist. Record your intake and expenditure. Make it a lifestyle and watch the pounds disappear with a mathematical formula.

Good luck!

Dietary Fiber in Foods

Food	Serving	Dietary Fiber (Grams)
Meats		0.0
Eggs		0.0
Milk & Milk Products		0.0
Fats (dressings, mayo.,etc.)		0.0
Vegetables:		
Corn on the cob	1 ear	5.9
Spinach (cooked)	1/2 cup	5.7
Corn off the cob	1/2 cup	4.5
Peas (boiled)	1/2 cup	4.2
Sweet potato	1 small	3.5
Broccoli	1/2 cup	3.2
Baked potato w/skin	1 med.	3.0
Boiled potato peeled	1 med.	2.7
Eggplant (cooked)	1/2 cup	2.5
Brussels sprouts	1/2 cup	2.3
Carrots, raw	1 med.	2.3
Carrots, boiled	1/2 cup.	2.3
Avocado	1/2	2.2
Beets, boiled	1/2 cup	2.1
Tomato	1 med.	2.0
Cabbage, boiled	1/2 cup	2.0
French fries	10	1.6
Lettuce	1/6 head	1.4
Asparagus	4 spears	0.9
Mushrooms, raw	1/2 cup	0.9
Mashed potatoes	1/2 cup	0.9
Celery, raw	1 stalk	0.7
Beans:		
Baked beans	1/2 cup	11.0
Chili w/beans	1/2 cup	8.5
Kidney beans	1/2 cup	4.5
Lima beans	1/2 cup	1.4

Common High Fat Foods

	Calories Per Serving	% Calories From Fat	Total Calories From Fat
Dairy:			
Cheddar Cheese (2 oz.)	228	73	166
Swiss Cheese (2 oz.)	214	73	156
Eggs (2 large)	164	64	105
Cream Cheese (2 Tbsp.)	89	58	78
Whole Milk (8 oz.)	139	47	75
Ice Cream (1/2 cup)	95	48	46
Fish:			
Herring (4 oz.)	235	39	139
Sardines (4 oz.)	230	49	111
Mackerel (4 oz.)	204	50	102
Sockeye Salmon (4 oz.)	194	49	95
Meat:			
Pork, Boston Butt (4 oz.)	275	53	146
Pork, Loin Roast (4 oz.)	287	50	144
Hot Dog (2 oz.)	176	80	141
Beef, Rib Roast (4 oz.)	273	50	137
Beef, Club Steak (4 oz.)	277	48	133
Liverwurst (2 oz.)	174	75	131
Lamb Chops (4 oz.)	239	45	108
Nuts and Seeds:			
Almonds (2 oz.)	246	77	189
Walnuts (2 oz.)	196	79	155
Sunflower Seeds (2 oz.)	200	71	142
Peanut Butter (2 Tbsp.)	188	71	137
Baked Goods:			
Apple Pie (1 slice)	302	38	115
Danish Pastry (1/8 ring)	179	49	89
Croissant (one)	109	30	55
Others:			
Avocado (1/2)	188	82	154
Coconut (1/2"x 2" piece)	156	53	133
Milk Chocolate (1oz.)	147	53	78

Sample Meals

Meal #1 (High Fat)	
Item	Calories
Fried Chicken (3 1/2 oz.)	265
Sautéed Vegetable (1 cup)	115
Baked Potato w/ Sour Cream & Butter	260
Salad with 2 Tbsp. regular dressing	295
Whole Milk	170
Biscuits (2)	200
Butter (2 tsp.)	90
Total Calories	1395
Calories from Fat	972
Percent of Calories from Fat	70%

Meal #2 (Low Fat)	
Item	Calories
Broiled Chicken (3 1/2 oz.)	193
Steamed Vegetable (1 cup)	25
Baked Potato w/ Chives only	100
Salad with 2 Tbsp. low fat dressing	60
Nonfat Milk	90
Whole Wheat Bread (2)	160
Butter (1 tsp.)	45
Total Calories	673
Calories from Fat 1	89
Percent of Calories from Fat	28%

GOALS AND ACTIVITIES FOR THE WEEK OF:

_____ to _____

Partners and Contact Numbers:

My Visions Are	
	Family
	Spiritual
	Physical
	Business/Financial
	Educational
	Recreational

My Number One Priority for Accomplishments this Month Is:	My Key Goal for this Month:

	My Promises/Goals for the Week are:	p/g
1		
2		
3		
4		
5		
6		
7		
8		
9		
10		
11		
12		
13		
14		
15		
16		
17		
18		

Weekly Call Sheet

Day: _____ **Date:** _____

	Calls	Time	Contacts	Calls	Time	Contacts			
							1	11	21	31	41
							2	12	22	32	42
							3	13	23	33	43
							4	14	24	34	44
							5	15	25	35	45
							6	16	26	36	46
							7	17	27	37	47
							8	18	28	38	48
							9	19	29	39	49
132							10	20	30	40	50

COULD
YOUR
CAREER
USE A COACH?

Reprint from: Executive Female
Article by: Carol Wheeler
September/October 1995

No self-respecting tennis player would do without one. Why should you?

Why does a busy executive in a communications conglomerate in Texas clear her calendar at the same time every week for a 30-minute executive coach, the one person with whom she can share all the disasters and triumphs of her professional life and, in the process, get career guidance. (It doesn't hurt her private life, either.)

Executive coaches used to be as rare as private washrooms. They were for CEO's and presidents only. But luckily, in the '90s, with careers more complicated than ever, that's no longer the case. Paula Day Caldwell, an executive at AT&T in Florida, swears by the process. She was having some trouble balancing a fast-track career with her roles as wife and mother of two young children. "Coaching has not only made an overall improvement in my life," she says. "It has also helped me challenge my associates to be all they can be. Some days I don't know what I'd do without Susan."...

At Caldwell's division at AT&T, the belief in coaching is so strong that bosses aren't called bosses anymore: Caldwell herself is a "coach" instead of a boss (she's a sales manager, and the people who report to her are her "associates." Traditionally, she says, a sales manager's job would have been simply managing sales and people. "But now the key is developing your people, helping to identify their growth areas, their developmental areas and then coaching them through so they are more self-sustaining, more independent employees." Caldwell uses the techniques she learned from Corbett to coach her own people...

ZEROING IN ON THE PROBLEM

The women in executive positions who come to Dee Soder, a prominent New York City coach, might be wondering if they've hit a glass ceiling. "Or is it me?" they ask themselves. Soder, whose firm, Endymion, puts her clients through an exhaustive battery of psychological tests of her own devising, pores over the story of their life (this writing project is a client's first assignment and then comes her professional conclusions. Just writing the autobiography (Soder has received everything form "ten single-spaced pages to two spiral bound notebooks") and enduring the testing can tell the seeker a lot, but it's followed by up to eight hours of feedback from Soder, zeroing in on the subject's strengths and weaknesses and how they may affect success in the workplace, Soder, ...describes her job as "helping successful people become more successful..."

BEING THE BEST YOU CAN BE

Coaching is having a dedicated mentor; it's getting knowledgeable support and encouragement and a new way of looking at things when you need it. As Susan Corbett puts it, "When you look at fine arts and sports, you see people using coaches to inspire them to go beyond the ordinary, to bring out their best. In every activity that involves performance, coaching can play a critical role." So why not business? Surely it's also crucial in the workplace to get help being your best...

Val Williams, a former psychotherapist who is now a coach in New Jersey, says that she uses "some of the same techniques" she used in psychotherapy but that coaching is "more skills-based, much more of a partnership. Instead of focusing on the past and on how you feel about it today, you focus on what skills you need today to create the future, or the present, you want." Williams says this is why she likes coaching; "It's about having a life that's more than just working.' Her clients, she says, are "a lot like me - in their 30's and 40s, successful but wanting more."...

YOU HAVE TO BE READY

Not everyone is coachable, however, says Susan Corbett. "You have to be ready to invest in yourself." Corbett and her clients (most of them are entrepreneurs and lawyers) work together to decide on the best career goals to work toward. "We have a process, " she says, "to determine whether these are goals the client really wants or just goals they think they should want." Like any skilled coach, Corbett doesn't always get results by following a straight line. The kind of time management she teaches, for instance, focuses on providing for plenty of free time. "Most people think, well, I'd better get into action," she says. "That's not necessarily what's needed. There's a direct correlation between the amount of free time you take and the sharpness and creativity of your ideas and productivity," says Corbett.

Some clients seeking executive coaching need a different kind of help, and coaches are quick to refer those with unrelated or additional problems to the right professional - whether it's a psychotherapist or a financial planner.

What seems to have democratized coaching is the telephone. Face-to-face consultation is often too expensive or too time-consuming for anyone but the very highest executives in a corporation or the most successful of entrepreneurs. But telephone coaching can work just as well.

Dee Soder, who works with those in the highest corporate echelons as well as artists, doctors, lawyers and middle managers, requires that her in-depth assessment process be done face-to-face. But she is totally comfortable with telephone follow-up thereafter. Soder even has a private emergency number for clients in a hot spot. When a call comes through on that number, everything else stops while she answers. .....

PRIVATE EXECUTIVE DEVELOPMENT

Who couldn't use this kind of mentor? Corporations can be daunting places, even for the successful manager—not the sort of setting where you bare your soul to your peers, let alone your boss. Coaching is a lot more private. Michael H. Frisch, Ph.D., director of coaching, serves in the Northeast for Personnel Decisions, Inc. (PDI), says coaching is "executive development, delivered one-on-one." Nevertheless, Frisch contends that "there'll always be some stigma when people ask for help." But Paula Caldwell at AT&T is happy to talk about being coached, as are Susan Gauff in California and many others. In any case, if you hire your own, there's no need to mention it to anyone else. As for entrepreneurs and sole practitioners, they make their own rules and, as Susan Corbett puts it, "Everyone goes to them for help; where do they go?"

Frisch's firm provides personal coaching only at the highest level, often involving the employee's boss and colleagues in goal-setting and progress reports. PDI is usually hired by a company's human resources department to provide executive development services.

How does Frisch get results? "Executives are complicated people," he says. "You need to use sophisticated methods to achieve progress." PDI's program includes simulations, role-playing, testing and teaching. By and large, he says, "it's going to be management, solving problems collabora-tively, fostering open dialogue."

WHAT WILL IT COST?

Coaching doesn't come cheap — if you can get it as a perk, go for it. If not, consider this; it's an investment that could be worth its weight in promotions. Coaches such as Susan Caldwell, charge in the range of $200-300 up to $500 per month for weekly half-hour phone sessions. Dee Soder charges $3,000 to $5,000 for a full assessment and feedback; after that there's an hourly fee for coaching. Alternatively, she offers a package of $10,000 to $15,000 all-inclusive for six months. And Personnel Decisions, Inc. (PDI) charges approximately $20,000 an exec-utive for the complete programs. As Michael Frisch says, "For a company, it can be a lot cheaper than finding a new executive team."

WHO NEEDS A COACH, ANYWAY?

According to Dee Soder, "Women often err on the side of trying to do too much by themselves. The common perception is that men don't ask for advice. But that's not always true. Guys see it as I'm going to win this thing. I am going to make the most money. And I'll do anything it takes, whether it's coaching or whatever." Some of the reasons you might want to try coaching are:

❑ You're beginning to feel you're in over your head.

❑ You can't decide on what seems like a great new job offer.

❑ You find that your yelling and screaming quotient is on the rise.

❑ You wonder if you've hit a glass ceiling.

Finally, if you're caught in a downsizing, coaching could be a lifesaver. Out placement firms often offer the service, so fight for it in any severance package you negotiate.

For most of us, coaching is a perk worth getting, whoever pays.

San Jose Mercury News
WEDNESDAY
APRIL 19, 1995

PERSONAL ZEST

More and more people are hiring coaches - once the purview to execs - to help cope with life's stresses

BY ALAN GATHRIGHT
Mercury News Staff Writer

LIKE many players in the frenzied and unpredictable working arena of the '90s, Donna Trombly dragged herself home from work feeling frazzled, listless and daunted about tomorrow's contest.

A veteran executive assistant with Hewlett Packard in Palo Alto, Trombly was struggling to find her groove a year into a new assignment. And after making the hour-plus home commute over winding, mountainous Highway 17 to Aptos, she sometimes found herself nodding off when she and her husband went out to enjoy some jazz.

But instead of throwing in the towel, Trombly got her employer to hire a personal coach, Melanie Gadener of Productivity Plus in Fremont.

"Now, I'm vitalized at the end of the day. I feel a lot more grounded and secure within myself. It's given me tools that I can use in every part of my life."

Personal coaching — once a perk confined to high-level executives — is now expanding to help folks with everyday life. People ranging from an independent photographer in San Francisco to a computer software engineer in Mountain View are hiring personal coaches to help balance career and private lives, to push them out for morning jogs, or to inspire them to pursue their most long delayed dream.

In a sense, personal coaches are professional nudges for the '90s, gently prodding people to stop dithering and just do it. Clients say coaches bring out their best by helping them focus, break down tasks and clarify their values.

Personal coaches say they differ from therapists in that they're not giving advice or trying to heal emotional problems. Instead, they keep clients on track toward their goals and talk them through "stops."

Indeed, there is no formal qualification or training needed to become a personal coach. These "lifestyle" coaches come from varied backgrounds. Some were psychologists, others business consultants, others stress-management counselors. Some have a degree; some don't. All say they share this one philosophy:

"As a coach, you hold (people) accountable for the priorities and commitments they have made for themselves and help them work through obstacles," Gadner says.

Began at the top

It's a phenomenon that started in the corporate boardroom in the 1980s, when a few executives would hire costly personal coaches to give them that extra edge over competitors. But as the rest of us have taken to enlisting coaches, their service has evolved into many variations with vastly different prices. Today, regular folks can get a half-hour of personal coaching over the telephone for as little as $25 a week, or splurge and command a coach's personal attention at $250 an hour. Many coaches require a minimum three- to six-month commitment, because - as they say—"change takes time."

While some coaches specialize in fitness or professional issues, others advise people about everything from controlling their spending to finding Mr. or Mrs. Right.

But in this age of company downsizing and shaky job security, coaches say many people are seeking greater control over their livelihoods, and more time for private pursuits and family.

"People are asking, 'Why should I put up with working for someone else 60 to 80 hours a week if I could be out on my can next year?'" says psychologist Jeffrey Wildfogel, who offers " achievement coaching" at his Mountain View firm, the Mental Edge Inc.

Fulfillment

"I'm having more and more people saying, 'I don't want to be a better salesperson or manager or small business owner. I want a more fulfilling life, and I want to switch careers,'" he says. "A lot of coaching is helping them develop the courage to do what they really want to do."

San Francisco advertising photographer John Lund says his career was stagnating five years ago before coach Laura Whitworth helped him recognize that he wanted to become a specialist in using computer manipulation to create eye-grabbing images. Now, he's internationally renowned for his advertising images of flying pigs and jockeys carrying horses around the racetrack.

"She helps me dig down deep in myself and come up with solutions for daunting problems," says Lund, 43. "She can take a task that seems overwhelming and help you break it down into doable steps."

For example, when Lund was puzzling over how to pay for his first computer equipment, Whitworth suggested starting with a low-end model computer and purchasing equipment for it with an advance from his first client. She also helped him develop a weightlifting routine and shed pounds.

Lund says he has more incentive to take definitive action when he and his coach have agreed on specific steps - and a telephone session with her looms.

"I've been through therapy and to me coaching is a more concrete kind of thing," he says. "A coach says, 'Here are the five steps you need to take.' A therapist is likely to say, 'Well how do you feel about this?'"

Coaches also help their charges decide which tasks require their best effort and which do not. "I've had to really battle the feeling that I wanted to do everything perfectly," Trombly says. "I've learned when something is enough. You have to be able to release things."

The right choice

Scott Shoffner, a 36-year-old Mountain View software engineer, say he was miserable about clashes with his boss. Then San Mateo coach Aaron Parnell used role-playing to show him how to gain the emotional detachment to resolve the dispute. He also learned that he was unhappy toiling in research and development. Parnell helped him see that he wanted to work closely with customers so he could see their satisfaction in using his software.

A shy man, Shoffner gained confidence in more than work: He has also begun dating regularly. "It's been quite the revelation."

Wildfogel, at the Mental Edge Inc., teaches clients that personal values, purpose and mission are just as important as talent. Too often, people give up when the road gets rough because they are unwittingly chasing a goal that's more important to their parents or peers than it is to them.

"So maybe you have the talent, but that's not enough if it's not what you really want to do," says Wildfogel.

Use care when selecting a personal coach

Picking a personal coach is a challenge in itself because the developing field has no formal training. Coaches come from backgrounds that include psychology, stress management, productivity consulting, and even massage therapy.

The San Francisco-based International Association of Professional and Personal Coaches was formed 17 months ago to help develop professional and ethical standards for coaches, says Aaron Parnell, a San Mateo coach and co-chairman of the association.

Parnell's background is typical of personal coaches' eclectic experience. Before becoming a coach, Parnell worked as massage therapist at the 1984 Summer Olympics, a personal trainer and stress counselor.

"What really matters is our ability to connect with a client and cultivate their ability to achieve," he says. "Our effectiveness speaks for itself."

But THE COACHES Training Institute in San Francisco is formalizing these skills with weekend seminars and a seven-month coaching certification course, says San Francisco coach Laura Whitworth, a former accountant who co-founded the school.

Coaches say consumers should ask all coaches for references and a listing of past work experience. Consumers should also pick coaches whose styles match their needs. Techniques vary from the "task master" who stands over you until you get it done to the "conceptual coach," who can give different perspectives on ways to achieve your goal.

If you're not sure you want to hire a coach, but do want to test out the idea, you can try a group course. The Soquel-Capitola Communities Activities program offers "Exercise Adherence" and "Stop Procrastinating" for $12 to $14.

COACHING SKILLS GLOSSARY

Accountability:
Accountability is having your client account for what they said they were going to do. Accountability is determined by three questions: *1) What are you going to do? 2) By when will you do this? 3) How will I know?* Accountability does not include blame or judgment. Rather, the coach holds the client accountable to the client's vision or commitment and asks the client to account for the results of the intended action and, if necessary, define new actions to be taken.

Acknowledgment:
Acknowledgment addresses the self and who the client had to be in order to accomplish whatever action they took or awareness they achieved.
"I acknowledge the courage that it took for you to show up on this call, knowing that you had some difficult things to share with me today."

Articulating:
Telling the client what you see them doing: repeating or mirroring back to them what they have just said to you.
"You are really working hard at this project and it is frustrating for you that your partners are not working as hard as you are."

Asking permission:
This is a skill which enables the client to grant the coaching relationship the access to unusually intimate or sometimes impolite areas of focus.
"Can I tell you a hard truth?" "Is it alright to coach you on this issue?" "Can I tell you what I see?"

Bottom-lining:
This is the skill of brevity and succinctness on the part of both coach and client. Bottom-lining is also about having the client get to the essence of their communication rather than engaging in long descriptive stories.
"I came to work this morning and was distraught when I found a pink slip in my box."

Brainstorming:

The coach and client generate ideas, alternatives and possible solutions even though some of the proposed ideas may be outrageous and impractical. This is merely a creative exercise to expand the possibilities available to the client. No attachment exists on the part of coach or client to any of the ideas suggested.

Celebrating:

Celebrating fully honors the place where the client currently experiences him or herself in life. The coach uses this skill to deepen the client's appreciation of the client's successes and failures, disappointments and wins. Celebrating is not necessarily about cheering. Rather, it is about bringing attention and acknowledgment to the client's process.

"You failed to make ten cold calls this week. I celebrate your failure."
"Hooray! I celebrate your success of getting a new client."

Challenging:

Challenging is requesting that a client stretch way beyond their self-imposed limits. Frequently, in the face of a challenge, the client will respond with a counteroffer that is greater than they would have initially allowed themselves to make otherwise. For example, a client needs to make cold calls to increase business. They think that they can only make one call a day and you challenge them.

"I challenge you to make ten calls a day!"

Champion:

When you champion a client, you stand up for them when they doubt or question their abilities. Despite the client's self-doubt, the coach knows clearly who the client is and that the client is capable of much more than the client thinks. When the client is in the valley, the coach is on the next hill, waving a flag saying, "Come on. You can make it!"

Clarifying:

When clients are unable to articulate clearly what they want or where they are going, the coach clarifies their experience. Clarification may be used in response to a client's vague sense of what they want, confusion or uncertainty. This skill represents a synergistic application of questioning, reframing and articulating what is going on. It is particularly useful during the intake process.

Clearing:

Clearing is a skill of benefit to both client and coach. When a client is pre-occupied with a situation or mental state which interferes with their ability to be present or take action, the coach assists the client by being an active listener while the client vents or complains. This active listening allows the client to temporarily clear the situation out of the way and to focus on taking the next step. When a coach gets hooked by a client interaction or is preoccupied by issues that do not pertain to the client, the coach can also share their experience or preoccupation with another colleague or friend in order to show up and be fully present with their client.

Client's agenda:

The client's agenda consists of the client's Life Purpose, Vision, Values, Goals and the Principles of Fulfillment, Balance, and Process. In short, it is everything that the client is and wants to be and do.

Confidentiality:

<u>All</u> information that a client shares with a coach is held as confidential. This means that all information that a client confides in you is <u>not shared with anyone else</u> without the client's expressed permission. Confidentiality, the hallmark of the coaching profession, creates safety and trust and is the basis of the powerful designed alliance between client and coach.

Creating trust:

The coaching relationship rests on a foundation of safety and trust. To create trust a coach might discuss safety, maintain confidentiality, tell the truth, offer the client an opportunity to ask for what they want, and actively listen to what the client is telling the coach.

Dancing in the moment:

Dancing in the moment means being completely present with the client, holding your client's agendas, accessing your intuition, and letting your client lead you. When you dance in the moment, you are open to whatever steps your client takes and are willing to go in the client's direction and flow.

Designing the alliance:

When the client grants power to the alliance, the client takes responsibility for his or her part of the alliance. Out of their ownership of the alliance, the client designs the alliance that will be most beneficial to and supportive of forwarding their actions toward their goals and vision. This is done through making requests of the coach, setting up the logistics of the coaching relationship, and discussing the best ways to facilitate client learning and action.

Forwarding the action:

This skill utilizes all other coaching skills with an added emphasis on moving the client forward. It may be through bottom-lining so that something gets done during the session. Forwarding the action may occur through bringing the client back to the focus of a goal, or through reframing something in such a way that the client is free to take action. Powerful forwarding the action occurs when a coach has the client DO IT NOW during the coaching session. This provides immediate support and immediate celebration once the action is taken. *Acknowledging* a client can also forward action.

Goals:

A goal is an outcome that the client would like to achieve. Goals are most helpful when they are measurable, specific, are owned by the client, have a date by which they will be accomplished, are made public (in order to achieve support and accountability), and constitute a reasonable stretch for the client.

Holding the client's agenda:

Holding the client's agenda is both a philosophical stance and a skill employed by coaches. When a coach holds the client's agenda, the coach becomes invisible, that is, the coach lets go of opinions, judgments and answers in support of facilitating the client's fulfillment, balance, and process. The coach follows the client's lead without knowing the RIGHT answer, without giving solutions or telling the client what to do. Holding the client's agenda requires coaches to put their whole attention on the client and the client's agenda, not on the coach's agenda for the client.

Holding the focus:

Once the client has determined a direction or course of action, the coach's job is to keep the client on track and true to a chosen course. Frequently, clients will be distracted by events in their lives, strong feelings elicited by the ALIEN or the mere wealth of other possibilities available. The coach consistently reminds clients of their focus and assists them in redirecting their energy back to their desired outcomes and life choices.

Inquiry:

An inquiry can be posed as a powerful question or request during the coaching interaction. When answered, it will usually result in a decision or a commitment to a future action. A powerful question might be as simple as *"How can this be avoided next time?"* A request might be *"Will you mail your brochure by Friday?"*

When an inquiry is used as homework at the end of the session, it is intended to deepen the client's learning and provide further reflection. The intention is for the client to consider the inquiry between sessions and to see what occurs. The inquiry is usually based upon a particular situation that the client is currently addressing.
"What are you tolerating?"
"What is challenging?"

Intrude/Take Charge:

On occasion, the coach may need to intrude, to interrupt or wake up a client who is going on and on, or who is kidding themselves. Sometimes the intrusion is a hard truth such as *"You are kidding yourself."* Sometimes the intrusion is simply stating what is going on, such as, *"You are skirting the issue."* Intrusion is considered rude in American society. THE COACHES Training Institute views intrusion a speaking straight to the client, allowing the client to honestly assess and directly deal with situations.

Intuiting:

Intuiting is the process of accessing and trusting one's inner knowing. Intuition is direct knowing, unencumbered by our thinking mind. The process of intuiting is non-linear and non-rational. Sometimes, the information received through intuiting does not make rational sense to the coach. However, this information is usually quite valuable to the client. Intuiting involves taking risks and trusting your gut.
"I have a hunch that..."
"I wonder if..."

Life balance:

Life balance is dynamic and is always in motion. Clients are either moving toward balance in their lives or away from balance. The job of the coach is to facilitate moving toward life balance as much as possible. The areas to be balanced in life generally include career, money, relationships, family and friends, romance, personal growth, fun, recreation, health, and physical environment. If one or more areas is receiving attention at the expense of the others, life will feel unbalanced and bumpy.

Life purpose:

Life purpose is about why a person is here on the planet. Questions may be: *"Who is it that you are moved to be?"* or *"What is it that you are moved to create?"*

Listening:

The coach listens for the client's vision, values commitment, and purpose in words and demeanor. To "listen for" is to listen in search of something. The coach listens with a consciousness, with a purpose and focus that comes from the alliance that is designed with the client. The coach is listening for the client's agenda, not the coach's agenda for the client. THE COACHES Training Institute calls it Level 1 when listening to your own thoughts, judgments and opinions, while *"listening for"* is Level 2, and *"conscious listening"* is Level 3.

Metaphor:

Metaphors are used to illustrate a point and paint a verbal picture for the client. *Your mind is like a ping pong ball bouncing between one choice and another. You're almost at the finish line. Go for it! You can win the race!*

Meta-view:

Meta-view is the big picture or perspective. The coach pulls back from the client's immediate issues and, from the clarity of that expanded perspective, reflects back to the client what the coach sees.

Planning and Goal-Setting:

The coach helps clients articulate the direction that they wish to take and actively monitors the progress made by clients. Clients can frequently benefit from support in planning and time management as coaches help them develop their skills in these areas.

Powerful Questions:

A powerful question evokes clarity, action, discovery, insight or commitment. It creates greater possibility, new learning, or clearer vision. Powerful questions are open-ended questions that do not elicit a "yes" or "no" response. Powerful questions are derived from holding the client's agenda and either forward the client's action or deepen their learning. Examples of powerful questions are:

"What do you want?" or,

"What does that cost you?"

Reframing:

Reframing involves providing a client with another perspective. When a coach reframes a situation, he or she takes the original data and interprets it in a different way.

A client has just been informed that he or she was selected as second choice for hire to a high-powered position in a very competitive market. The client is disappointed and is questioning his or her own professional competence. A reframe of the situation is: To be chosen as second choice in such a competitive market indicates the high quality of your expertise and experience.

Requesting:

One of the most potent coaching skills is that of making a request of the client. The request, based upon the client's agenda, is designed to forward the client's action. The request includes a specified action, conditions of satisfaction, and a date or time by which it will be done. Four possible responses to a request are: 1) "Yes," 2) "No," 3) a counteroffer, or 4) agree to a future time that a response will be given.

"Will you pay your telephone bill by Friday?"

Self-management:

Self-management is the ability of the coach to become invisible in the service of holding the client's agenda. This means to put aside all opinions, preferences, judgments, and beliefs in order to reflect and support the client's agenda. Another facet of self-management includes managing the client's "gremlin." The coach can aid the client in identifying the "gremlin" and then providing tools that the client can use in managing their "gremlin."

Structures:

Structures are devices that remind the client of their vision, goals, purpose or actions that they need to take immediately. Some examples of structures are collages, calendars, messages on voicemail, alarm clocks, etc.

Values:

Values represent who you are right now. They are principles that you hold to be of worth in your life. People often confuse values with morals. Values are not chosen; they are intrinsic to you.

Vision:

This is a multi-faceted mental image and set of goals which personally defines and inspires the client to take action to create that picture in their actual life. A powerful vision is sensuous, exciting and magnetic, constantly attracting the client's desire to bring the image to fruition. Vision provides the client with a direction and can provide meaning in the client's life.

ADDITIONAL AIDS FOR SUPER ACHIEVEMENT
AND PERFORMANCE

BAROQUE MUSIC—Largo Movements
A collection of the slower, 60-beats-per-minute largo movements of baroque music for use in making your reinforcement tape.

1 cassette	1 CD
$13.00	$17.00

MISSION ACCOMPLISHED
The entire Human Performance Training program recorded in a studio without time constraints and containing all of the available researched and practical information on how to make and use your baroque-music monthly goals tape. If you can't get to the live training program or if you have attended and want to bring the program home in even greater detail, this is the series for you!

8 cassettes and workbook
$78.00

HOW TO OVERCOME PROCRASTINATION: CONFUSION TO CLARITY.
Learn how to overcome procrastination by empowering yourself with the distinctions of time wasted through avoidance of psychological prisons of the "I have to's" and learn the true meaning of FOCUS. Also presented in this album is Bob Davies at his best in a presentation talking about handling stress with Rational Emotive Style. You will have a reinforcement tape made for you included in this series using the power of baroque music. This will enable you to condition yourself to use the information in this series effortlessly.

3 cassettes and workbook
$38.00

SELF-IMAGE, VISUALIZATIONS AND MINDMAPPING
We have been conditioned to think, feel, and act the way we do. Some of it is good for us and protects us, and some of it is harmful and limits us. Knowledge is power. We have become so accustomed to speaking and writing words, we mistakenly assume that normal sentence structure is the best way to remember images and ideas. Now you can learn how to use both sides of your brain to remember information as well as how to put fun back into learning.

2 cassettes
$24.00

THE SUBCONSCIOUS ASPECTS OF PERSUASION
Appeal to a client's subconscious mind to break habitual ways of thinking by using precise language. Included is an explanation of personality types and how to sell them. You will also learn human communication, the creation of rapport, precision probing, and understanding how to sell an idea or product in the way your client likes to buy!

4 cassettes
$45.00

LIVING A HEALTHY LIFESTYLE

This series clearly addresses the issue of controlling a habit such as overeating by exploring the role of food in our lives. You will learn the difference between hunger and appetite. You will experience a TOTAL program with proven results. This series contains new information about diets and breakthrough research on how to make your body an efficient energy-burning machine!

10 cassettes and workbook
$85.00

SENSORY GOAL SETTING

The human brain has been compared to a hologram by Dr. Carl Pridbram of Stanford. Learn how to neurologically encode high achievement traits the neurolinguistic programming (NLP) way.

1 cassette
$13.00

CIGARETTE SMOKING

Learn the latest techniques of habit control—emphasizes the dangers and addictions of smoking and some outstanding nuts and bolts of how to rid yourself of a controlling habit for good!

1 cassette
$13.00

THE SKY IS NOT THE LIMIT: YOU ARE!

The book by Bob Davies that covers everything he does in his seminars plus a lot more! It is a thorough examination of how your mind works and how you can make it work to achieve your goals in every area of your life and includes detailed instructions for creating your own mind maps. Also included is a complete step-by-step guide to making your own reinforcement tape, how to choose an accountability partner, and how to make partnering work for both of you!

Book
$15.00

COACHING FOR HIGH PERFORMANCE

Eighteen Essential Elements for Professional and Personal Coaching

This book creates a structure for professional and personal coaching. After reading this book, you will have the competency to coach another person for focus, clarity, accountability, increased fulfillment, and productivity. These skills are immediately useful. (Worksheets and forms are included.)

Book
$15.00

151

Order Form

TITLE	QTY.	EACH	SHIPPING WEIGHT	TOTAL
Baroque Music Tape / CD		13.00 / 17.00	2 ounces	
Mission Accomplished		78.00	1 pound	
How To Overcome Procrastination		38.00	1 pound	
Self-Image, Visualization, Mind Mapping		24.00	10 ounces	
Subconscious Aspects of Persuasion		45.00	1 pound	
Living a Healthy Lifestyle		85.00	2 pounds	
Sensory Goal Setting		13.00	2 ounces	
Cigarette Smoking		13.00	2 ounces	
The Sky Is Not The Limit. You Are!		15.00	1 pound	
Coaching For High Performance		15.00	1 pound	
			Subtotal	
			Sales Tax (Calif.)	
			Shipping and Handling	
			Total	

Shipping And Handling: All orders shipped via ground UPS. Shipping charges: $4 for the first pound + $1 for each additional pound or portion. (For example; 3 pounds, 2 ounces = 4 pounds = $5 shipping).

Payment by: _____ Check _____ Credit card

(circle one) Visa   Mastercard   AmEx

Card Number: _____ Exp. Date: _____

Name on Card: _____

Signature _____

Name _____
Street _____
City _____ State _____
Phone # _____
(Necessary for credit card orders)

PHONE IN OR FAX YOUR CREDIT CARD ORDER FOR SAME DAY SHIPMENT!
Phone: 949-223-3704 Fax: 949-830-9492

High Performance Training Inc. 20992 Ashley Lane, Lake Forest, CA 92630-5865

NOTES:

NOTES

NOTES

NOTES

NOTES